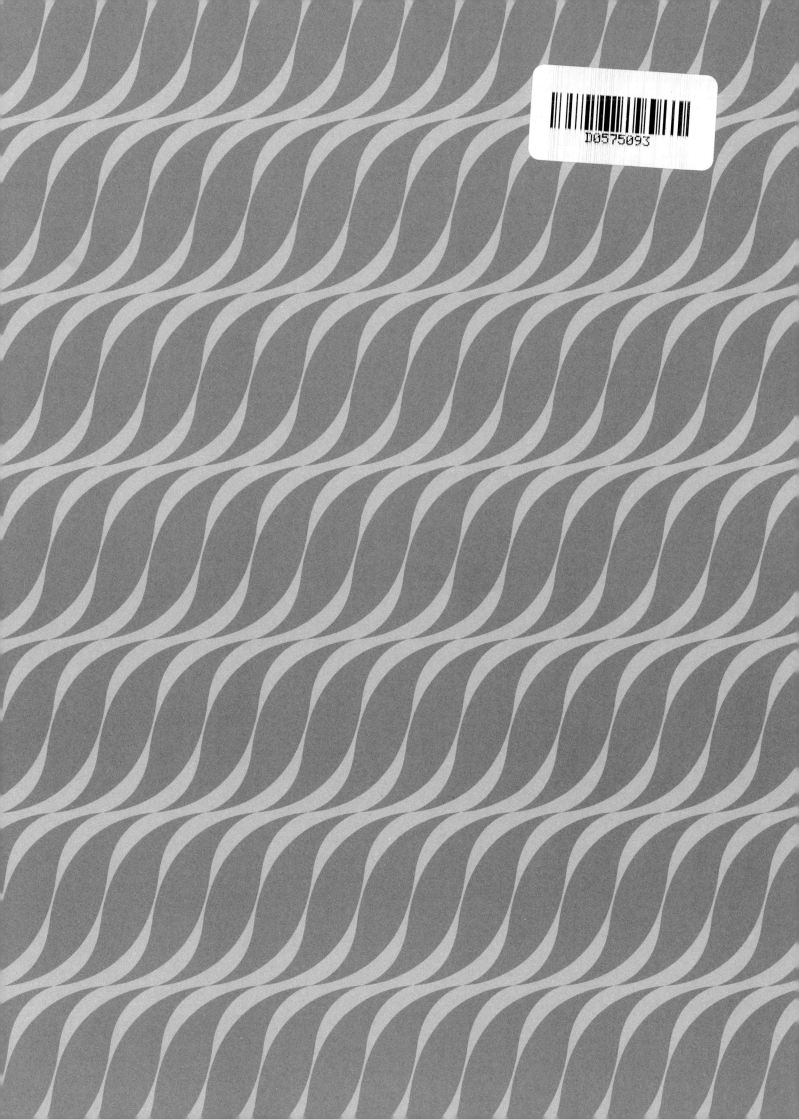

GREAT
RAILWAY JOURNEYS

GREAT

RAILWAY JOURNEYS

Legendary train routes of the Western World including North America, South America, Canada and Europe

Max Wade-Matthews

southwater

This edition is published by Southwater
Southwater is an imprint of
Anness Publishing Limited
Hermes House
88-89 Blackfriars Road
London
SE1 8HA
tel. 020 7401 2077
fax. 020 7633 9499

Distributed in the UK by
The Manning Partnership
251-253 London Road East
Batheaston
Bath BA1 7RL
tel. 01225 852 727
fax. 01225 852 852

Distributed in the USA by
Anness Publishing Inc.
27 West 20th Street
Suite 504
New York
NY 10011
tel. 212 807 6739
fax. 212 807 6813

Distributed in Australia by
Sandstone Publishing
Unit 1, 360 Norton Street
Leichhardt
New South Wales 2040
Australia
tel. 02 9560 7888
fax. 02 9560 7488

© 1998, 2000 Anness Publishing Limited

1 3 5 7 9 10 8 6 4 2

Publisher Joanna Lorenz
Project Editor Joanne Rippin
Editor Emma Gray
Designer Michael Morey

Contributors George Beherand, Tom Ferris, Frank Hornby, Alan Pike, Graham Pike, Christopher Portway,
Brian Solomon, Kenneth Westcott-Jones, Max Wade-Matthews, Neil Wheelwright

Previously published as part of a larger compendium, *Great Railway Journeys of the World*

● **ABOVE**
Several interurban cars gather at East Troy, Wisconsin, USA.

● **HALF TITLE PAGE**
Boone & Scenic Valley's Mikado takes on water on a hot June day, Iowa, USA.

● **FRONTISPIECE**
Part of the coastal section of the London Paddington to Penzance line, England.

● **TITLE PAGE**
The Agawa Canyon train tour crossing the Montreal River by a trestle bridge, Canada.

CONTENTS

● **ABOVE**
No. 4498 Sir Nigel Gresley travelling under a bridge near Ais Gill.

Introduction

This book will take the reader from the thrilling 3,200 km (2,000 mile) trip from Chicago to Oakland in North America to the 27 km (17 mile) jaunt back in time between Bedford and Bletchley in rural Bedfordshire, England. We will ascend the high mountains of Peru and Switzerland; and descend under the English Channel as we travel through one of the wonders of the modern world – the Channel Tunnel.

Rail journeys for pleasure began in the late nineteenth century with growing prosperity and the adoption of the workers' holiday. In many parts of Europe and America are to be found towns that came into prominence in the latter half of the nineteenth century for the simple reason that they had the good fortune to find themselves connected to the growing railway network. Many of the journeys detailed here are still in operation; others, however, are now part of history and can only be travelled in the pages of a book such as this.

● **OPPOSITE**
A summer view of the train from the Look-out in Agawa Canyon, Ontario, Canada.

● **ABOVE**
Superliners in Amtrak's Chicago coach yard.

TORONTO TO VANCOUVER

Only one transcontinental train journey for passengers is still operating across Canada, over a length of 4,467 km (2,776 miles). This is from Toronto to Vancouver by the Canadian National route under the auspices of the VIA Rail Corporation.

The train runs three times a week as the Canadian, a name taken over from Canadian Pacific, which inaugurated it in 1954 with the first streamlined sleeper train in Canada. Three days and three nights are spent by the Canadian on its journey, which is a mixture of tour land-cruise and point-to-point transportation. Passengers in the former category pay quite large sums for superior accommodation and brilliantly restored public rooms and diner.

Although transcontinental trains used to run from Montreal, the starting-point

for the journey today is Toronto, and the route lies by way of Capreol (close to Sudbury, Ontario), then across hundreds of kilometres of pre-Cambrian shield to Sioux Lookout, later winding through the Manitoba Lake District to Winnipeg, 1,958 km (1,217 miles) from Toronto. After a stop of one hour, the Canadian heads west across rolling prairies to Saskatoon, Saskatchewan, and Edmonton, Alberta, before climbing into

● **TOP**
An exterior view of Vancouver's Pacific Central railway station.

● **ABOVE LEFT**
An interior view of one of the Canadian's domed park cars. From these seats, passengers can drink in the full beauty of the diverse Canadian countryside.

● **LEFT**
VIA's Canadian on the tracks of the Canadian Pacific between Montreal and Vancouver.

● **LEFT**
The east-bound Canadian, *en route* from Vancouver
to Toronto, takes a break at Banff, Alberta.

● **BELOW**
The concourse of Toronto's Union Station.

the foothills of the Rocky Mountains.

Jasper is high amid these mountains,
and here the train halts for 70 minutes
while some of the cars are attached to the
Skeena, which has come from Edmonton
on its way to the Pacific at Prince Rupert.
The main part of the Canadian carries on
through the Rockies, going over Yellow
Head Pass and down to Kamloops. The
final part of the journey is beside the
Fraser River (with the tracks of the
Canadian Pacific Railway on the opposite
bank) down to Vancouver, which is
reached at 08.30 Pacific Time on the
third morning after leaving Toronto.
Inevitably some of the best scenery is
passed at night, but the high points of the
Rockies are viewed in daylight. At one
time, Canada had three transcontinental

routes, which it could not support
economically. These came down to two
when Canadian National was formed
from earlier private systems (Grand
Trunk, Canadian Northern and Grand
Trunk Western). As recently as 1967
there were four transcontinental trains
each day, all from Montreal.

While air competition hurt these
trains, the greatest damage was done by
the completion of the Trans-Canada
highway in 1968, leading to the
reduction in service to just one train
thrice weekly. However, thanks to
support from tour operators in the USA
and particularly Britain and Germany, the
Canadian now seems profitable in its new
dual role as tour train and short-haul
passenger service. For tour passengers,
meals in the refurbished diner, use of the
vista domes, lounges and sleeping cars
newly equipped with showers, are
included in the fare.

● **ABOVE LEFT**
The Canadian leaves Montreal's Windsor
Station on the first part of its journey across
the Canadian continent.

● **LEFT**
The Canadian winds its way through a
background of autumnal colour.

INFORMATION BOX

Termini	Toronto and Vancouver
Country	Canada
Distance	4,467 km (2,776 miles)
Date of opening	1885

SAULT SAINTE MARIE TO HEARST

Running from south to north across Ontario, the Algoma Central & Hudson Bay Railway (ACR) is a private company dating from 1899. The starting-point is Sault Sainte Marie (known as the Soo) at the eastern end of Lake Superior, the world's largest lake. Its main line, 476 km (296 miles) long, ends at Hearst, still more than 240 km (150 miles) from the sub-Arctic bay. It passes through mountains that are the highest in Canada

INFORMATION BOX

Termini	Sault Sainte Marie and Hearst
Country	Canada
Distance	476 km (296 miles)
Date of opening	1899

east of the Rockies. The daily passenger-train threads its way through a landscape of canyons, forests, lakes and fast-flowing rivers. On spring, summer and autumn weekends, this is the longest and busiest passenger-train on the North American continent.

The great train runs as an excursion because so many people want to visit Agawa Canyon in the heart of Algoma Country. While about three cars continue to Hearst, another 18 to 20, including the restaurant cars and one diesel

locomotive, are uncoupled and stay on the floor of the canyon for about two hours. Hikers and picnickers can enjoy the area until the southbound train from Hearst arrives to join up the heavy load, hook on the waiting diesel and run back to the Soo, 183 km (114 miles) to the south. Originally the railway was built for iron-ore traffic coming from the Helen Mine near Michipicetin, to which a branch was extended, while the main route to Hearst sought to carry general freight, especially lumber.

● **RIGHT**
The train snakes
through the
autumnal beauty of
the Agawa Canyon.

● **BELOW**
As well as travelling in the public coaches,
passengers can also hire their own car. Here is
one of the private cars – "Michipicoton" –
which was built by Pullman of Chicago in 1910.

● **BELOW RIGHT**
The train also runs in
winter, the warmth of
the coaches keeping
the ice and sub-zero
temperatures at bay.
Here we see it making
its way through the
deep snow.

spectacular trestle affords stupendous
views. There is a twisting climb to
Hubert, 461 m (1,512 ft) above sea level
and the summit of the line.

While the section to Agawa Canyon
carries holidaymakers *en masse*, the
northern part of the line numbers big
game hunters and fishermen among its
customers. In the autumn, when foliage
colours are fantastic, and moose and deer
are "in season", the train, which stops on
flag request along the way, is called the
Moose Meat Special.

The Algoma Central possesses 25
diesel locomotives painted in maroon,
cream and grey, while the passenger cars
are in a very attractive maroon.

Although it is allied to the Algoma
Steel Corporation, the railway is a
separate entity and enjoys steady
profitability. A large proportion of
Algoma Central's profit comes from its
well-advertised passenger service. It is
not unusual for 1,200 to 1,500
passengers to ride to Agawa Canyon on a
summer Sunday, paying about $30
Canadian (£14) each for the excursion.

It helps that there are no roads
competing with the railway, except at
Hawk Junction, 265 km (165 miles)
from the Soo. The line's isolation is
interrupted at two points: Franz, where
there is a junction with Canadian
Pacific's main line (now freight only), and
Oba, where the Canadian National
crosses it. Both are hamlets, and only at
Oba, a flag stop, can a change be made
for passengers when VIA's Canadian
comes through three times a week.

Great rivers are crossed on fine trestle
bridges, including those over the Goulais,
South and North Chippewa, and the
Batchewana. The biggest of these crosses
the Montreal River at Milepost 93. This

VANCOUVER TO SQUAMISH

● **BELOW**
Preserved ex-Canadian Pacific Royal Hudson
class locomotive No. 2860 at Squamish. This
4-6-4 locomotive was built in 1940 by the
Montreal Locomotive Works.

The route from North Vancouver to
Squamish is on the British Columbia
Railway (known as BC Rail or BCR),
which is primarily a freight railway. The
section travelled is, at 61 km (38 miles),
only a small fraction of the company's
network, which totals over 2,172 km
(1,350 miles). Passenger services are
limited to a daily service each way
between North Vancouver, Lillooet and
Prince George. The train named the
Cariboo Prospector, takes 13 ½ hours to
travel 745 km (463 miles). In addition,
there is a school train between Seton
Portage and Lillooet. In the summer
months, there are two tourist-oriented
services: a weekday service north from
Whistler and the Royal Hudson service
described here.

The BCR, which was called the Pacific
Great Eastern Railway until 1972,
connects to the Canadian National railway
(CN) and so to the rest of the Canadian
rail network at North Vancouver Junction.
There is also a connection to the
Vancouver Wharves Railway, which, as its
name implies, serves the port area.

The section of line from Squamish to
Vancouver only opened in 1956, quite a

● **LEFT**
The Royal Hudson
train, soon after
departure from
North Vancouver,
seen from Prospect
Point. Lions Gate
Bridge is just out of
sight to the right.

● **LEFT**
BCR diesels 4642＋762＋4615 at the north end
of Squamish yard waiting to depart on a
northbound freight. No. 4642 is a 4400 HP
General Electric DASH 9 built in 1995; 762 is a
3000 HP General Motors SD40 of 1980; 4615
is a General Electric 4000 HP DASH 8 of 1990.

INFORMATION BOX

Termini	Vancouver and Squamish
Country	Canada
Distance	61 km (38 miles)
Date of opening	1956

● LEFT
Shannon Falls seen from the water, a couple of miles south of Squamish.

while after the railway reached Squamish from the north. This was because the railway's main purpose was to link the logging and mining areas with the sea, and there are port facilities at Squamish for large bulk carriers. The BCR has expanded relatively recently, with the

● BELOW
Royal Hudson No. 2860 passing Porteau Cove in June 1996. The road, known as the Sea to Sky Highway, runs close to the line for most of the way from Horseshoe Bay to Squamish and provides several excellent photographic opportunities.

construction of a 132 km (82 mile) electrified branch (the Tumbler subdivision) in 1983.

The Royal Hudson runs Wednesdays to Sundays from June to September and takes two hours for the northbound trip. The train is named after the class of steam locomotive used to haul it, a type which were built by the Montreal Locomotive Works in 1939 for the Canadian Pacific Railway. Hudson is the name for the locomotive's wheel arrangement, 4-6-4. The Royal prefix comes from the occasion when one of the class (No. 2850) was used to haul the royal train during a visit of King George VI and Queen Elizabeth to Canada in 1939. Upon withdrawal, 2860 became the property of the British Columbia

Government, who currently lease it to BCR. In addition, BCR leases the 2-8-0 3716, built by MLW in 1912 for Canadian Pacific, as a reserve for these trains. Locomotive No. 2860 is resplendent in polished maroon and black, with a polished, unpainted metal-clad boiler and firebox, and royal crowns on each side above the cylinders.

The journey starts from BCR's North Vancouver station (depot). Adjacent to the station is the small shed used to store and maintain the steam locomotives. Across the tracks, there are extensive freight-yards and a diesel locomotive

depot. The train is made up of 12 coaches, mostly ex-CN stock of 1954, painted Tuscan Red. In the middle is an open-sided observation coach named Britannia, which was built in 1920. In June 1996 the weather was too chilly for all but the hardiest of passengers! The last vehicle is a parlour car, called Mount Cascade, which can be used on payment of around twice the normal fare.

The train leaves the station slowly, heads west and passes the freight-yards. At the end of these, it passes under the approaches to Lions Gate Bridge. This

was reputedly built with money from the Guinness brewing family to help in opening up the north shore, where they owned land. An excellent photographic location is the viewing area at Prospect Point on the Stanley Park Drive on the opposite bank, close to the bridge. The line keeps a short way from the waters of English Bay as it passes through residential areas and skirts Ambleside Beach. It then passes through the 1,280 m (4,200 ft) Horseshoe Bay tunnel, cutting off the "corner". Leaving the tunnel, the train heads north for the remainder of the journey. Just visible is the Horseshoe Bay ferry terminal, used by car ferries to Vancouver Island. Soon after this, the railway comes back down to the water's edge and rarely leaves it before reaching Squamish. Across the Sound there are views of great forests and snow-capped peaks.

The line, while curving considerably, is largely flat with only short gradients. The highest point is in Horseshoe Bay tunnel, 51 m (167 ft) above sea level, around 16 km (10 miles) out. Between North Vancouver and Squamish, there are passing-points at Brunswick, Porteau and Britannia.

• **LEFT**
A BCR track patrol vehicle passing Porteau Cove. This precedes the Royal Hudson by around five minutes to ensure that the line is free from such obstructions as fallen rocks.

downtown area, away from the main line. Squamish is home to the BCR workshops and main locomotive depot, and has a large area of sidings. It is also the home of the West Coast Railway Heritage Museum, which is by the north exit to the yards, a couple of kilometres from where the Royal Hudson stops. For those interested, there is a bookable add-on coach excursion to visit the museum during the Royal Hudson's layover.

The town of Squamish, population around 12,000, is not a tourist destination. However, it is a regional centre with a wide range of small shops and pleasant restaurants. The town is overshadowed by towering, rocky hills, those to the east being part of Garibaldi Provincial Park, the 816 m (2,677 ft) Mount Garibaldi being around 19 km (12 miles) to the north. The valley of the Cheakamus River, which drains into Howe Sound at Squamish, heads north to Whistler amid increasingly mountainous scenery.

At Porteau, the railway skirts a small bay in which some old ships have been scuttled to provide interest for divers. Porteau is also one of the best photographic locations. Eight kilometres (5 miles) further on, at Britannia Beach, there is the British Columbia Museum of Mining, at what was the largest copper producer in the British Empire. The scar on the scenery caused by the mine is visible from a considerable distance.

At Squamish, the Royal Hudson is reversed on to a siding adjacent to the

• **ABOVE RIGHT**
BCR Budd diesel railcar BC-33, built in 1957, at BCR's North Vancouver station soon after arrival on the southbound Cariboo Prospector.

• **RIGHT**
The lighthouse at the confluence of Howe Sound and English Bay, with the skyline of downtown Vancouver in the background.

WHITEHORSE TO SKAGWAY

The White Pass and Yukon Railway has had a chequered history. That history, however, is an integral part of the story of this exciting land, just as much as that of the great Canadian Pacific, and riding this down-to-earth line is one of northern Canada's great experiences.

The 177 km (110 mile) narrow-gauge railway connects Yukon's capital, Whitehorse, to the historic port of Skagway and the coastal shipping that calls there. In doing so the line passes through the territory of Yukon, British Columbia and Alaska. It was constructed to transport thousands of gold seekers and their supplies from Skagway through the coastal mountains to the beginning of the river route to the Klondike gold fields. Work began in May 1898, and the railway's last spike was driven at Carcross on 29 July 1900, the conclusion of 26 months of blasting, chipping, shovelling and hardship suffered by construction crews whose number fluctuated from 700 to 2,000. A narrow, moss-filled

INFORMATION BOX

Termini	Whitehorse and Skagway
Country	Canada
Distance	177 km (110 miles)
Date of opening	1900

● **ABOVE LEFT**
A photograph of the interior of the passengers' parlour car.

● **LEFT**
A view of the line stretching into the horizon.

● **BELOW LEFT**
A train passing through woodland on the descent to Skagway.

ledge beside the track, marked by a stone inscription, is a mute reminder of the trudging steps of the thousands of men and women who succumbed to the lure of gold.

When the gold rush died away, the Yukon population dwindled; and during the dark days of the 1930s, the trains operated only once a week, but the steam locomotives and the rotary ploughs kept the line open. Afterwards the line was used by tourists as well as for the transportation of ore; when some of the vintage parlour cars of 1883 were still in use. They made strange bedfellows with the heavy steel mineral wagons and multiple diesel locomotives that formed the rest of the trains. Then it became a goods-only line for a period. Today, only

● **RIGHT AND FAR RIGHT**
Views of the trackside, from the cab, as the train heads north.

● **BELOW RIGHT**
The track reaches its maximum height at Log Cabin, BC.

the route between Skagway and the half-way point of Bennet is used by tourists, mainly those from cruise ships.

Probably no tunnel in the world was built under greater difficulties than the one that penetrates a perpendicular barrier of rock, which juts out of the mountains like a giant flying buttress some 16 km (10 miles) north of Skagway. A short distance from the summit of the pass, a deep canyon is spanned by a steel cantilever bridge, 66 m (219 ft) from the creek's bed. Below, in Dead Horse Gulch, winds the old White Pass Trail, worn into the native rock by thousands of Sourdough boots. To improve the grade and curvature of the railway, both bridge and tunnel were replaced in 1969, but the originals still stand. From sea level at Skagway, the line climbs to the summit of the pass, 879 m (2,883 ft), in 34 km (21 miles). The highest point of the line is Log Cabin, BC, which is at an altitude of 889 m (2,917 ft).

From terminal to terminal, the journey takes about eight hours, and the views of the mountains and lakes are superb. Just 64 km (40 miles) from Skagway is a frame building called the

Bennet Eating House, where trains from both directions used to meet. Here passengers descend to sit down to a lunch, included in the ticket, of stew, beans, sourdough bread and apple pie.

THE SAN FRANCISCO MUNI

San Francisco is one of America's most scenic and most compact cities, and it is famous for its eclectic flavour and wonderful weather. The San Francisco Municipal Railway – better known as just the Muni – operates the city transit system, an integrated network of buses, electric buses (trolley coach), light rail, light-rail subway (Muni Metro) and the world-famous cable-cars. The Muni is one of the best ways to experience the city, and most of San Francisco is within a four-block walk of a transit line.

The Muni's cable-car routes are the most interesting rides in the city. The cable-car originated in San Francisco as a way of moving people by rail over its

● ABOVE
RIGHT
Muni PCC 1056 is painted in the scheme used by streetcars in Kansas City, Missouri. Like all the cars in regular service on the F-Market line, this PCC came from Philadelphia, Pennsylvania.

● RIGHT
A Boeing-Vertol LRV pops out of the Muni Metro on to Duboce Street. This J-Church car will take the turn on to Church. N-Judah cars also use this portal, but continue due west on Duboce up into the Sunset Tunnel and then to the Pacific Ocean.

exceptionally steep hills. There were many different routes operated by several companies. While other American cities also operated cable-cars, including New York City, Chicago and Seattle, today only San Francisco's remain. The three cable-car routes are a big tourist attraction, and at the peak tourist season it is not unusual to wait an hour or so to ride. The Powell & Hyde line is the most interesting line and the most popular. Both the Powell & Hyde and Powell & Mason routes begin at the corner of Market and Powell Streets near the downtown area. The Powell & Hyde line runs to Fishermans Wharf, passing through Chinatown and over both Russian Hill and Nob Hill. The best time to ride the cable-cars is on an early weekday morning in the winter. While you'll need a warm jacket, you might find yourself the only rider on the car! A vastly more attractive prospect than fighting the summer noontime hoards. The cable-cars are a very pleasant way to view the city, and are fun to ride.

The Muni operates six light-rail lines, five of which use modern equipment and feed into the Muni Metro subway downtown. The remaining route is the F-Market line, which runs from the Transbay bus terminal downtown along Market Street to Castro using historic PCC (Presidents' Conference

INFORMATION BOX

Terminus	San Francisco
Country	USA
Distance	48 km (30 miles)
Date of opening	1873

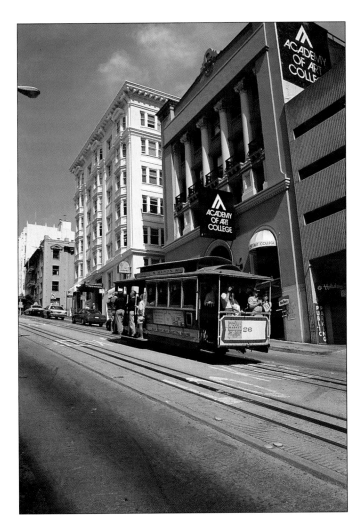

San Francisco's extraordinarily steep hills are the reason for the cable-cars: no conventional form of transport could negotiate these grades successfully. A Powell & Mason car rolls past the San Francisco Academy of Art on Powell Street in downtown San Francisco.

● **ABOVE**
Interior of a rebuilt PCC used on the F-Market line.

● **BELOW**
The San Francisco skyline at sunrise.

30th Street. Some cars turn back here, while others continue to Balboa Park via San José Avenue on a new line opened in the early 1990s. At present the Muni has a fleet of ageing Boeing-Vertol light-rail vehicles — an unsuccessful design used only in San Francisco and Boston — but it has a fleet of new Breda LRVs on order.

Committee) cars. In the early 1990s the Muni acquired secondhand PCCs from Philadelphia, had them rebuilt and painted each one differently. Each car wears the colour scheme of an American city transit system that once ran PCCs. One car is painted for Boston, another for Kansas City, etc. These cars entered regular revenue service on the F-Market route in 1995. The differently coloured cars make quite a spectacle coming up the street and are well worth riding.

Of the five light-rail lines operating into the Muni Metro, the J-Church line is the most interesting. It leaves the subway at Duboce and Church Streets, then follows Church for several blocks before winding up a steep grade on a private right of way through Dolores Park, which offers a spectacular view of the San Francisco skyline. The line rejoins Church after cresting the hill and runs to

CHICAGO TO SEATTLE
THE EMPIRE BUILDER

James J. Hill was a giant of American railroading. Small in stature, one-eyed and bearded, he was described by the legendary Lucius Beebe as piratical. By 1901 he was in control of three railroads, which served the then wilderness of the Pacific Northwest: the Great Northern, the Northern Pacific and the Burlington. These became known as the Hill Railroads. His crack train was the Oriental Limited, which ran from

INFORMATION BOX

THE EMPIRE BUILDER

Termini	Chicago and Seattle
Country	USA
Distance	3,575 km (2,222 miles)
Date of opening	1901

Chicago and the Twin Cities (Minneapolis-St Paul) to Seattle, where his own steamships linked the Pacific North-west to Japan and China. Much later, in 1929, when the Asiatic connection had faded, a splendid transcontinental train was named for him as the Empire Builder.

The Great Northern Railway worked as a separate entity to the Northern Pacific Railway, which also served Seattle

from the Twin Cities. But by 1971, with the coming of the quasi-nationalized Federal Corporation AMTRAK, only the Great Northern route – closest to the Canadian border – carried a passenger-train. This is still called the Empire Builder and is arguably the finest transcontinental ride in the States.

Since 1980, the train has been composed of the latest "superliner" equipment with day coaches, diner, sightseeing lounge and sleeping cars, all 5.2 m (17 ft) above track level. The first 687 km (427 miles) from Chicago to St Paul are over the Burlington. From St

● **RIGHT**
A view from the
Empire Builder as it
heads through
Flathead River
Indian Reservation,
Montana.

● **RIGHT**
A view from the
Empire Builder as it
heads through
Flathead River
Indian Reservation,
Montana.

● **OPPOSITE
FAR LEFT**
Amtrak's eastbound
Empire Builder
passes through
Grizzley, Montana,
against a backdrop
of the Rocky
Mountains.

● **OPPOSITE
LEFT**
An Amtrak
Superliner coach,
part of the Empire
Builder at Chicago
Union Station.

● **BELOW**
Amtrak's eastbound Empire Builder
approaches its station stop at Columbus,
Wisconsin.

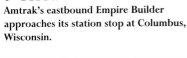

Paul it is 2,888 km (1,795 miles) to
Seattle, making a total journey of 3,575
km (2,222 miles).

From the start at Chicago's Union
Station there is a smart run to
Milwaukee, beer capital of America.
Then the train follows the Mississippi
River almost all the way to the Twin
Cities, with enchanting daylight views of
the great river on its upper reaches. The
really wide open spaces begin soon after
Minneapolis. In the small hours of the
first night, there is a stop at Fargo, the
town where the firm of Wells-Fargo –
the forerunner of today's American
Express – was founded. Next morning
the train passes Rugby, a flag-stop, where
there is an obelisk outside the station
marking the exact centre of the North
American continent.

After passing over yet more plains,
through Glasgow and Havre, the train
reaches Browning, Montana, where the
Rocky Mountains begin in dramatic style.

As the train climbs, passengers see to the
north a 2,500 m (8,000 ft) mountain
known as Triple Peak Divide, from which
the melting snows run off to three oceans
– the Atlantic, Pacific and Arctic. The
Empire Builder proceeds through the
scenic wonderland of Glacier National
Park, crossing the Continental Divide at
Marais Pass, which, at 1,596 m (5,236 ft),
is the lowest summit of any rail route

through the Rockies. James Hill sent a
surveyor called John Paul Stevens to find
out if this legendary low pass really
existed. Travelling alone, the first white
man to enter the region, he found it in
bitter winter weather. A statue of Stevens
may be seen on the right-hand side of the
train going west.

There are more mountains and river
scenery to Spokane, "Capital of the
Inland Empire", where the Portland,
Oregon, portion is detached. On the way
to Seattle, the main train passes through
the 12.5 km (7 ³/₄ mile) long bore of
Cascade Tunnel – the longest in the
Western Hemisphere – which was
opened in 1929. Breakfasting passengers
experience the train winding down from
Washington's Cascade Mountains and are
often treated to views of elk and deer on
the final stretch towards Seattle.

● **LEFT**
Marais Summit on the
former Great
Northern main-line in
northern Montana
hosts Amtrak's Empire
Builder and 30 to 40
daily Burlington
Northern Santa Fe
freight-trains. The
larger-than-life statue
is of John P. Stevens,
the man who surveyed
the line in the late
19th century.

PUEBLO TO DURANGO
THE SAN JUAN EXPRESS

● **BELOW**
A 16mm "fisheye" view of C&T Class K36 No. 487 with passenger-train behind at Chama, New Mexico.

The Denver and Rio Grande Railroad had the largest 36 in gauge system in the United States and even operated a sleeping-car and dining-car train over a 534 km (332 mile) route as the San Juan Express. This ran until the beginning of the 1950s from Pueblo, Colorado, via Alamosa, Colorado, and through northern New Mexico to Durango, south-western Colorado.

Some of this track remains and is operated by steam-trains over two sections – the 72 km (45 mile) Durango to Silverton, and the 103 km (64 mile) Antonito to Chama, New Mexico. The former line was run for many years as a tourist route by the Rio Grande before passing into private hands, and has become the foremost preserved line in America, with patronage from the public increasing year by year. The Antonito to

Chama line is a joint undertaking of the states of New Mexico and Colorado, leased to Kyle Railways.

A useful fleet of 2-8-2 locomotives survived the sad time when diesel engines replaced steam all over the nation, and nine splendid steam engines in sound order work the lines. The coaching stock on the Durango-Silverton line is partly original, while the Chama-Antonito line

level. From the train windows in this area, one can look down to see a cattle drive, with horsemen and countless steers, moving through a valley, looking no bigger than ants.

Durango is over 1,800 m (6,000 ft) up, and the line to Silverton climbs all the way through the San Juan mountains, at its most spectacular in the Animas Canyon, to reach nearly 2,750 m (9,000 ft) at the chilly old silver-mining town (which is how Silverton got its name). The train journey to Silverton takes about 3 ½ hours through the wilderness. The train waits at Silverton for 2 ¼ hours before returning downhill to Durango in about 15 minutes faster.

On the Cumbres and Toltec trip, some 6 ½ hours are spent travelling one way, including a picnic lunch stop at Osier near the summit. Both for this open-air venue and for travel in gondola cars, passengers must wrap up warmly, even in summer. The westbound train is called Colorado Limited, and the eastbound is called New Mexico Express. Return trips are made by buses the same day or the next day by train.

uses converted boxcars. As many as three trains each way daily are run on the Silverton line in peak season, with one a day at other times of the year, apart from around Thanksgiving in November to the New Year when there is no service, apart from one holiday train, until the spring snow melts. There is a daily train over the Chama-Antonito line from mid-May to mid-October.

This is high-country railroading. The Chama-Antonito line, whose proper title is the Cumbres and Toltec Scenic Railroad, climbs over the Cumbres Pass to reach 3,055 m (10,022 ft) above sea

INFORMATION BOX

THE SAN JUAN EXPRESS

Termini	Pueblo and Durango
Country	USA
Distance	534 km (332 miles)
Date of opening	1876

Manitou Springs to Pike's Peak

● **BOTTOM LEFT**
The sign at Pike's Peak summit terminus.

● **BELOW**
A train waits at the summit of Pike's Peak.

In 1806, Army Lieutenant Zebulan M. Pike, a United States military surveyor, came across a dramatic Rocky Mountain peak in what was then unknown Colorado Territory. He never climbed it but "established" the height at 5,500 m (18,000 ft). Ten years later an army team did climb to the summit, which was found to be 4,300 m (14,110 ft). Seventy-five years later, a steam railway wound its way up with the aid of a cog.

Cog railways were an American invention, the first being the White Mountain Line up to the summit of Mount Washington in New Hampshire – a mere 2,134 m (7,000 ft), but the windiest place on earth. The Swiss engineer Niklaus Riggenbach was an apprentice during the construction in 1866. All trains up this pioneer cog line are still steam powered.

On the Pike's Peak climb, a steam locomotive pushed a car upwards, and remained in operation from the 1891 opening until final retirement in September 1958. From 1938 onwards, though, some of the climbs were shared with a curious petrol-powered (gasoline-powered) railcar, which only carried 24

INFORMATION BOX

Termini	Manitou Springs and Pike's Peak
Country	USA
Distance	14.3 km (8.9 miles)
Date of opening	1891

passengers compared to 50 aboard the steam car. Since 1964, Swiss-built diesel-electric units (each carrying 80 passengers) have been in use, at first two of them, but later joined by two more from the Winterthur builders. In 1973, the Swiss works produced two diesel-electric sets – the first articulated ones to be used on a cog railway. They carry 216 passengers, and the volume of traffic on a clear summer's day is shown by the fact that sometimes as many as 16 trains are run. The round trip is just under four hours and trains operate, subject to visibility, from May to October.

The Manitou and Pike's Peak Railway is standard gauge, starting from the resort town of Manitou Springs, at the mouth of Englemann Canyon, through which the cog railway begins its journey. The old Colorado Midland railway used to bring passengers close to the cog line's depot, but today they come by bus. In early days, there was also an interurban tramway from Colorado Springs.

Passengers bound for the summit see the retired old Baldwin Tank No. 5. All

● LEFT
Swiss units at Manitou Springs, the bottom
terminus of the railway.

4,300 m (14,110 ft) above sea level. This
is a desolate spot with limited shelter, and
it is the highest point reached by rail on
the North American continent. Exactly
14.3 km (8.9 miles) from the Manitou
Springs depot, the views on a clear day are
described by the cog company as "showing
the grandest scenery on the Globe".

The stopover is usually 40 minutes, by
which time the chilled and breathless
passengers, satiated with views that take
in Denver, 113 km (70 miles) away, and
most of the 30 Colorado Rockies' peaks,
which are higher than Pike's, must return
to the train. In August 1911, a man and
his wife failed to return, having taken a
short walk, inadequately clad. They were
found frozen to death.

the other steam engines have been saved
and dispersed to museums. At 2,003 m
(6,571 ft), the start is already quite high,
but on its way through the canyon the
gradient increases to 1:4, and at the first
station, Minnehaha, the line reaches
2,540 m (8,332 ft). Then comes Son-of-
a-Gun Hill, also at 1:4, to Halfway
House. Passing through Lion Gulch on
easier gradients, the railway attains the
3,048 m (10,000 ft) mark at Mountain
View, where a dramatic panorama unfolds.

The climb continues, twisting and
turning, past Grecian Bend, Big Hill and
Windy Point to reach Summit House,

● ABOVE
A train waits at the
summit of Pike's
Peak. Train services
operate from May
(depending on snow
conditions) to late
October.

● LEFT
Pike's Peak summit
terminus, which is
4,300 m (14,110 ft)
above sea level.

ST ALBANS, VERMONT, TO WASHINGTON DC
THE VERMONTER

Vermont is among the most beautiful and pastoral regions in the eastern United States. It is bordered on the east by New Hampshire and on the west by New York State. It is known for its dairy farms, its maple syrup and its ski resorts. Following the discontinuance of the nocturnal Montrealer in 1995, a train that had run between Washington DC and Montreal, Quebec, Amtrak began operating a daylight train between Washington and St Albans, Vermont. Appropriately named the Vermonter, the train is funded by the state, and it is one of the most popular new trains in the north-eastern United States. It features a distinctive baggage car carrying the name of the train, and stops at rural towns in Massachusetts, New Hampshire and Vermont. Without the train, these communities would have no public transport.

Between St Albans, Vermont, and Palmer, Massachusetts, the Vermonter operates over the New England Central, a short-line railroad run by RailTex, a large short-line operator based in Texas. The New England Central began operations in February 1995, only a few months before the Vermonter, on trackage that

On a cold winter's day, the Vermonter crosses the Quaboag River on the old Boston & Albany line. The Vermonter uses a short stretch of the old B&A between Palmer and Springfield, Massachusetts. A specially painted baggage car makes Amtrak's Vermonter particularly distinctive.

● ABOVE
The Vermonter pauses at Amherst, Massachusetts, on a sunny Sunday afternoon.

● BELOW
The southbound Vermonter approaches the short, narrow tunnel at Bellows Falls, Vermont.

was formerly operated by the Canadian National through its Central Vermont subsidiary. The Vermonter has the distinction of being one of the few daily Amtrak trains to operate over a short-line freight railroad (as opposed to a larger Class I railroad), and one of the few Amtrak trains to operate in "dark territory" — a section of track not protected by automatic block signals. This is not to say operations are casual or haphazard: a strict system of track occupancy authority is in place. The Vermonter safely shares the tracks with New England Central's couple of daily freights.

South of Palmer, the Vermonter operates to Springfield over Conrail's busy Boston Line — a route used by several

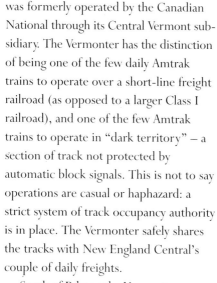

INFORMATION BOX

THE VERMONTER	
Termini	St Albans, Vermont, and Washington DC
Country	USA
Distance	975 km (606 miles)
Date of opening	1995

● **RIGHT**
The Vermonter,
Amtrak train No. 56,
runs swiftly along
the Connecticut
River backwater
near Vernon,
Vermont.

● **BELOW LEFT**
On New Year's Day
1997, the
southbound
Vermonter crosses
the high bridge at
Millers Falls,
Massachusetts.

● **BELOW RIGHT**
On a crisp clear
October afternoon,
the Vermonter
approaches
Amherst,
Massachusetts.

other Amtrak trains. From Springfield to New Haven, it uses the Springfield Branch of the North-east Corridor, and then follows the main stem of the Corridor – Amtrak's most travelled route – all the way to Washington. However, the most interesting section of the trip is the New England Central portion. The train stops in Amherst, Massachusetts, a small college town, and once the home of the famous poet Emily Dickinson. In Vermont, the train serves Brattleboro, Bellows Falls, Windsor, White River Junction, Randolph, Montpelier, Waterbury, Essex

Junction and St Albans. Bellows Falls is the site of a short tunnel, which passes directly below the town centre.

In the summer and early autumn, the Bellows Falls station is shared with the privately operated Green Mountain passenger-train which carries sightseers on a round trip to Chester, Vermont. Between Bellows Falls and Windsor, the tracks cross over the Connecticut River into New Hampshire, and the train stops at Claremont – currently the only point in the Granite State served by a passenger-train. From the train, passengers can see

Mt Ascutney, one of the tallest mountains in Vermont, and wooden-covered bridges, for which the region is famous.

The northbound train, No. 56, departs Washington in the early morning and arrives in St Albans in the evening, while the southbound train, No. 55, features the same schedule but in reverse. It arrives in Washington about the same time as its counterpart arrives in St Albans. The Vermonter requires reservations. Amtrak revises its schedules every six months, and prospective passengers should consult the carrier before riding.

BOSTON TO CHICAGO
LAKE SHORE LIMITED

The Western Railroad of Massachusetts – one of the first mountain railroads in the world – crossed the Berkshire Hills to connect Boston with the Erie Canal at Albany, New York. The line was surveyed by American railroad pioneer George Washington Whistler in the 1830s and completed in the early 1840s. To maintain a reasonable ascending grade on the east slope of the Berkshires, Whistler followed the course of the west branch of the Westfield River, crossing the river several times using large stone-arched bridges. Although the ruling westbound grade was kept to 1.67 per cent, on its completion it was one of the longest adhesion grades in the world. Especially powerful locomotives were required to bring trains through the hills.

In 1867 the Western Railroad merged with the Boston & Worcester to form the Boston & Albany, and in 1900 the New York Central leased the route. Ownership of the line has since changed several times, but to local residents it is known as simply the "B&A". Today, Whistler's railroad makes up the most scenic portion of the route traversed by the Boston

● **LEFT**
Amtrak's Lake Shore Limited climbs Springfield Hill against the dramatic backdrop of a brooding, stormy November sky.

● **BELOW LEFT**
One of George Washington Whistler's famous stone-arch bridges over the Westfield River, near Middlefield. This is one of several bridges abandoned in 1912 when the railroad was realigned.

section of Amtrak's Lake Shore Limited, trains 448 and 449. This train operates daily between Chicago Union Station and South Station in Boston, Massachusetts. Between Chicago, Illinois, and Rensselaer, New York, the Boston section is combined with the New York section.

Bound for Boston the Lake Shore leaves Rensselaer around lunch-time for a relaxing run over the Berkshires. To climb out of the Hudson River valley, the train uses a section of track to a junction at Post Road, which was abandoned in the early 1970s after Penn Central (then the owner of B&A) discontinued the passenger service. Since all freight traffic

INFORMATION BOX

LAKE SHORE LTD

Termini	Boston and Chicago
Country	USA
Distance	1,636 km (1,017 miles)
Date of opening	1840s

uses the Castleton Cutoff west of Post Road to Selkirk, the old passenger line to Albany was deemed redundant. However, after Amtrak reintroduced a passenger service, the old track was put back. East of Chatham, New York, the tracks pass over the New York State Thruway, and a short while later through the famous

● **LEFT**
Amtrak No. 448 exits from the east portal of the State Line tunnel on a clear summer morning. This famous short, curved tunnel is located only about a mile from the New York-Massachusetts state line.

direction on both tracks. On the east slope, near the village of Middlefield, several of Whistler's stone arches are visible through the trees on the north side of the tracks. These bridges were abandoned in 1912, when the railroad was realigned to reduce the gradient. At Chester, the remains of an engine facility, complete with roundhouse and cooling tower, can be seen on the south side of the tracks. The westbound run out of Boston is less revealing because, except in the long days of summer, the train unfortunately runs through the most interesting scenery at night.

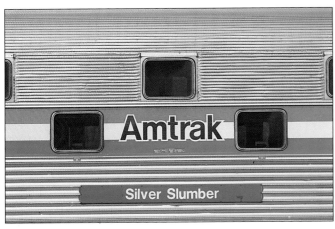

State Line tunnel – so named because it is located near the New York-Massachusetts state line. This is a twin-bore tunnel, although at present only the south bore is used. The north bore was abandoned in the late 1980s.

East of the station stop at Pittsfield, Massachusetts, the track begins the climb up to Washington Summit, elevation 445 m (1,459 ft) above sea level – the highest point on the old B&A. It is not unusual for the Lake Shore to overtake a slow-moving eastbound freight climbing the grade. The railroad is bi-directional double track over Washington Mountain, so trains may safely operate in either

● **ABOVE**
An Amtrak Heritage sleeping car, typical of those used on the Lake Shore Limited.

● **RIGHT**
Amtrak No. 448 winds down the grade on the east slope of Washington Hill, east of Middlefield, Massachusetts.

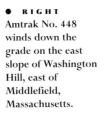

CHICAGO TO OAKLAND
THE CALIFORNIA ZEPHYR

Connecting Chicago and Oakland, California, is one of Amtrak's most popular western trains, the California Zephyr. On the way it traverses some of the most spectacular scenery in the West, from the towering Colorado Front Range to the California coast. It runs up around the "Big Ten curves" west of Denver, crests the divide via the famous Moffat Tunnel, runs through the deep rugged Gore and Glenwood Canyons, across the Utah Desert and over Soldier Summit to Salt Lake City. Then it passes through the Nevada deserts, over California's Donner Pass, across the Central valley and along the Carquinez Straits to Oakland.

While some routes may have a scenic highlight, the route of the California Zephyr is defined by the scenic splendour it passes through; it has not one highlight but rather a continual succession of great vistas. Among the best are those found when climbing high above the Plains up into the Front Range, where the city of

Denver is seen in the distance against a seemingly infinite horizon. However, the most spectacular view is on the west slope of Donner Pass. After crossing the Smart Ridge, which separates the Yuba River Basin from that of the American

River, the railroad follows the American River Canyon; while the river drops deep into the cavernous ravine, the railroad rides high on the north side, along the right of way laid out in the 1860s by the Central Pacific's chief supporter and

● **ABOVE LEFT**
Amtrak No. 5 crosses Yuba Pass after a winter storm. The City of San Francisco was snowbound at Yuba Pass for three days in the early 1950s.

● **LEFT**
The westbound California Zephyr crosses Smart Ridge, leaving the Yuba River Basin and entering the American River Basin, west of Donner Pass.

● **LEFT**
Amtrak No. 6 climbs along the Truckee River
at Floriston, California.

great visionary genius, Theodore Judah.
At American, just east of the village of
Alta, California, the tracks ride the very
edge of the canyon, 610 m (2,000 ft)
above the river. From this spot on a clear
night, the lights of Sacramento nearly
113 km (70 miles) away can be seen.

Although the original California
Zephyr began operations in 1949, this
train was discontinued in 1970. The
present-day California Zephyr uses much
of the original route, except that it goes
over Donner Pass rather than via Feather
River Canyon. Amtrak's reincarnated
California Zephyr began operation in the
mid-1970s, but did not start operation,

via the Denver and Rio Grande Western
line over the Front Range, until 1983. It
runs with Amtrak's typical western
equipment: the high-level Superliners,
which may be hauled by its ubiquitous
Electro Motive F40s (200-400 series), the
boxy General Electric P32 "Pepsi Cans"
(500 series) and the aesthetically
controversial streamlined General Electric
Genesis diesels (series 1-99 and 800s).

● **ABOVE**
Cosmic sunrise over Donner Lake in June
1990. Amtrak runs high above this serene
mountain lake on the right of way located by
Theodore Judah in the 1860s.

● **BELOW**
Amtrak No. 5 passes through the Colorado
Rockies on the Dotsero Cutoff – a line that
was finally completed in the 1930s to connect
the Denver & Salt Lake with the Denver & Rio
Grande Western.

INFORMATION BOX

THE CALIFORNIA ZEPHYR

Termini	Chicago and Oakland
Country	USA
Distance	3,218 km (2,000 miles)
Date of opening	1949

SEATTLE TO LOS ANGELES
THE COAST STARLIGHT

The Coast Starlight, connecting Seattle with Los Angeles, is Amtrak's premier West Coast train. It offers first-class accommodations and features splendid scenery all along its route. On the way it traverses several mountain ranges, including the Oregon Cascades and California's Coast Range, and south of San Luis Obispo, California, it runs along the Pacific Ocean for many miles. Amtrak advertises the Coast Starlight as "superior service": first-class passengers are treated in comfort to complimentary wine tasting and champagne.

South of Eugene, Oregon, at the village of Oakridge the Starlight begins its ascent of the Oregon Cascades. Southern Pacific completed its Cascade Route in the mid-1920s, when it opened its Natron Cutoff between Black Butte and Eugene. Today this is among the most impressively engineered lines in the West. A few miles out of Oakridge the tracks wind over a tall trestle at Heather, amid tall evergreen trees. The tracks twist their way up the mountain and pass through a series of long snowsheds and tunnels.

● **LEFT**
Amtrak No. 11, the Los Angeles-bound Coast Starlight, rolls down the Embarcedero at Jack London Square in Oakland, California. Two General Electric P32 diesel-electric locomotives, which are nicknamed "Pepsi Cans", lead the train.

● **BELOW LEFT**
Amtrak No. 11 climbs up through Cruzatte, Oregon – high in the Cascades – on its way to California from Seattle and Portland.

INFORMATION BOX

THE COAST STARLIGHT

Termini	Seattle and Los Angeles
Country	USA
Distance	2,235 km (1,389 miles)
Date of opening	1894

Near Cruzatte, the tracks pass from a tunnel into a snowshed, then out across a tall curved trestle over the cascading Noisy Creek, into another snowshed, then through a long curving tunnel. As breathtaking as the scenery is in the summer, it is downright awesome in the winter, when the trees are heavily laden with pristine snow, and the snowsheds protect the tracks from avalanche. Unfortunately, the southbound Starlight usually crosses the Cascades at night in the winter, although the northbound makes a daylight run.

Amtrak does not serve San Francisco directly, but instead provides a bus service from its new Emeryville Station. Passengers wishing to ride into San Francisco by rail can change for a Cal Train "commute" at San José. In Oakland, the Starlight runs down the Embarcedero through Jack London Square, where the train stops at Amtrak's new Oakland station. The street here is a memorable experience. There are few places where Amtrak's high-level Superliner cars share the right of way with automobile traffic! To reach San Luis Obispo from the agricultural Salinas

valley, the Starlight crosses the Cuesta Grade, a steep, tortuous 22.5 km (14 mile) stretch of railroad that winds its way through some of California's prettiest scenery: rolling grassy hills punctuated by perfectly placed oak trees. The grass is iridescent green for a few weeks in March and April, and golden brown for the rest of the year.

The ride along the coast brings the Starlight through Vandenberg Air Force Base, land otherwise restricted to militia. You will not find many photographs of the train in this isolated spot. North of

● **ABOVE LEFT**
Coast Starlight advertisement at the new Amtrak station in Oakland, California.

● **ABOVE RIGHT**
On a misty June day, the Seattle-bound Coast Starlight descends Southern Pacific's Cascade Line near Fields, Oregon.

Santa Barbara, the tracks pass over a tremendous trestle at Gaviota and along several popular beaches. The southern end point is Los Angeles Union passenger terminal, one of the last great American passenger terminals. It was completed in 1939 and blends Spanish-Moorish architecture with 20th-century Art Deco motifs.

● **ABOVE**
Amtrak's Coast Starlight has just passed through Tunnel 5½ in the Salinas valley. Before the tunnel was drilled the railroad ran around the mountain on a circuitous alignment (visible to the left of the tunnel).

● **LEFT**
The Pacific Ocean glints in the morning sun.

BELLOWS FALLS TO CHESTER, VERMONT
THE GREEN MOUNTAIN FLYER

The Rutland Railway once connected Bellows Falls, Rutland and Burlington, Vermont, with Ogdensburg, New York; it also had a line running south from Rutland to Bennington, Vermont, and on to Chatham, New York. The Rutland discontinued all operations in the early 1960s and portions of the line were abandoned.

Today the Green Mountain Railroad operates a segment of the former Rutland Railway, and a very short portion of the former Boston & Maine Railroad in south-central Vermont between North Walpole, New Hampshire (directly across the Connecticut River from Bellows Falls, Vermont), and Rutland, Vermont. This colourful short-line railroad maintains the spirit of the old Rutland Railway by using Rutland's shield and green and

● **LEFT**
The Green Mountain Flyer departs Chester, Vermont, bound for Bellows Falls.

● **LEFT**
The Green Mountain Railroad logo is reminiscent of the old Rutland herald.

● **BELOW**
On a brilliant autumn morning, Green Mountain Alco RS-1 405 leads the Green Mountain Flyer at Brockway Mills, Vermont.

● **RIGHT**
When the passenger-train is running heavy, it rates one of the powerful Green Mountain's GP9 locomotives.

● **BELOW RIGHT**
At the end of the day, the Green Mountain Flyer rests at Bellows Falls, Vermont.

yellow colour scheme on its rolling stock. From late spring through early autumn Green Mountain operates a tourist train called the Green Mountain Flyer.

The train runs twice a day on Tuesday through Sunday (daily in foliage season) between the Amtrak station in Bellows Falls (also serves the daily Vermonter) and Chester. The train runs with vintage passenger-cars including two historical former Rutland cars, still bearing the name of their former owner.

The Flyer is reminiscent of a typical backwoods branch-line passenger-train of an earlier period, giving passengers a refreshing change from the modern Amtrak trains that are most prevalent in the United States today. Green Mountain operates several Electro Motive GP9

diesel-electric locomotives, which it purchased secondhand from other railroads, as well as a vintage Alco RS-1 diesel-electric, which dates from the mid-1940s and was once owned by the Rutland. Often Green Mountain operates the Flyer with the RS-1, and the train appears even more the way a traditional Rutland passenger-train might have looked 50 years ago.

The scenery along the line is outstanding. Passengers may board the Flyer at either end of the line, and both Bellows Falls and Chester feature splendid stations. Leaving Bellows Falls,

the railroad briefly follows the Connecticut River and then winds its way inland. At Brockway Mills the tracks cross a deep gorge on a high-deck bridge. Along the way several of Vermont's quaint covered bridges and a number of old rustic barns are visible. Vermont is most enjoyable in the early autumn when the days are crisp and clear and the foliage turns to brilliant colours, and there is no better way to view the scenery than to ride the Green Mountain Flyer. Special trains are run on October weekends, the peak period for autumnal colours, all the way to Ludlow, Vermont.

INFORMATION BOX

THE GREEN MOUNTAIN FLYER

Termini	Bellows Falls and Chester, Vermont
Country	USA
Distance	21 km (13 miles)
Date opened for passenger traffic	1984

CHICAGO METRA'S "RACE TRACK"

Chicago's Metra operates a comprehensive network of suburban commuter lines with more than a dozen routes over half a dozen different railroads. Its busiest route is the former Chicago, Burlington & Quincy line to Aurora – a suburb about 56 km (35 miles) west of the the downtown area.

The route, known colloquially as the "Race Track", is owned by Burlington Northern Santa Fe. It carries approximately 50,000 weekday Metra

● RIGHT
An express makes a station stop at Stone Avenue, La Grange.

INFORMATION BOX

Termini	Chicago and Aurora, Illinois
Country	USA
Distance	61 km (38 miles)
Date of opening	1853

passengers on more than 80 daily commuter trains, handles several daily Amtrak long-distance passenger-trains, including the Southwest Chief and the California Zephyr, and carries between 40 and 60 daily freight-trains operated by host railroad Burlington Northern Santa Fe, plus those by Canadian National and Southern Pacific/Union Pacific.

The combination of heavy passenger-traffic and heavy freight-traffic makes this triple-track main-line one of the busiest in the United States, and one of the most interesting to watch and ride. Aurora-bound trains serve Chicago Union Station, one of four large passenger terminals in Chicago. The operation of the triple track is handled by Centralized Traffic Control, allowing trains to use all three tracks in both directions.

In the evening rush hour, when the bulk of passengers are leaving the city, local and express-trains depart Chicago Union every few minutes. Local trains normally use the outside track on the north side, while the express-trains use

● LEFT
An F40M "Winnebago" races westbound at Stone Avenue. These locomotives are unique to Chicago.

the centre track and inbound trains the outside track on the south side. To avoid interference during the peak passenger times, freight-trains are either held in yards in either Chicago or Eola, or west of Aurora.

Metra normally uses bi-level "gallery cars" hauled by Electro Motive Division F40s or F40Ms. The F40s are America's most common passenger locomotives, while the F40Ms – nicknamed "Winnebagos", after the popular motor

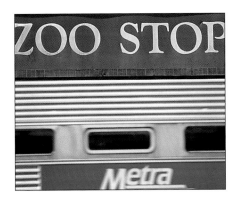

home – are unique to Chicago Metra. All Metra trains are operated in a push-pull fashion, with the locomotive facing westward. Eastbound trains are operated from a control cab in the leading passenger car. Running time between Chicago and Aurora varies from 1 hour and 20 minutes on a local run to just 52 minutes on an express train.

One way to enjoy the action on the "Race Track" is to ride a midday Metra train from Union Station to one of the

suburban stops – Hollywood (Brookfield Zoo) and Stone Avenue, La Grange, are recommended – and spend the afternoon watching the railroad. On a typical weekday, there will be plenty of freight- and passenger-trains. At weekends Metra service is limited. Other interesting Metra routes include: Metra Electric to University Park – the former Illinois Central electric lines; Rock Island District to Joliet, Illinois; and any of the three former Chicago & North Western routes.

MILWAUKEE TO EAST TROY

Beginning in the 1890s, interurban electric railways were in use across the United States. Employing relatively lightweight construction, they often operated along country roads and in city streets. A great many interurbans operated in the Midwest, connecting such large cities as Chicago and Milwaukee with rural outlying towns. In addition to their passenger operations, many interurbans carried freight, using small electric locomotives. However, the interurban era was short-lived. The advent of the automobile put a swift end to many of these marginally profitable lines, and most were abandoned in the 1920s and 1930s.

The Milwaukee Electric Railway & Light Company, which operated a 320 km (199 mile) long interurban electric empire in south-eastern Wisconsin,

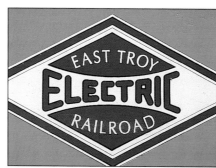

● **ABOVE**
The East Troy Electric Railroad serves several industries in East Troy by means of the Trent Spur. An excursion using open-bench car 21 celebrates the inauguration of electric service in 1996.

● **LEFT**
The East Troy Electric Railroad herald.

● **BELOW**
A car rolls through Beulah on its way from East Troy to the Elegant Farmer.

● **RIGHT**
One of East Troy's most popular cars is Duluth-Superior Transit "Gate car" No. 253, a typical American streetcar. The interior of the car has been meticulously restored.

● **BELOW LEFT**
Former Milwaukee Electric Railway & Light Company steeple-cab L9, and former Chicago, South Shore & South Bend interurban coach No. 1130 in front of the old substation, now a museum, at East Troy, Wisconsin.

● **BELOW RIGHT**
One of East Troy's interurban cars rolls through the Army Lake Road crossing near Mukwonago, Wisconsin. Much of this rural line follows the highway on the 8 km (5 mile) run between East Troy and Mukwonago.

● **BOTTOM**
A former Chicago, South Shore & South Bend interurban takes the siding at Beulah for two eastbound cars heading for the Elegant Farmer. This old interurban route is single track with passing sidings at several locations to allow "meets" between passing trains.

opened its line to rural East Troy, Wisconsin, in 1907. While Milwaukee Electric abandoned passenger service to East Troy in 1939, this line survived for many years as an electric freight line. The village of East Troy maintained the line to serve local industries. Today it is one of the last electrified remnants of the inter-urban era. It is operated by the East Troy Electric Railroad and provides weekend passenger excursions in conjunction with the Wisconsin Trolley Museum between May and September, using traditional interurban equipment. It is still a freight-hauler too, although in the 1990s it has only carried 20–30 cars per year.

Passengers may board at either East Troy or the Elegant Farmer, near Mukwonago, Wisconsin. The 16 km (10 mile) round trip runs along a county high-way through pastoral farming country and takes a little more than an hour. East Troy operates a fleet of vintage electric

interurban equipment, including cars that operated on the Chicago, South Shore & South Bend. It also operates streetcars from several North American cities, including Duluth, Minnesota and Philadelphia. The pride of its fleet is car No. 21, a single-truck open-bench

streetcar replica, typical of street railway operations at the turn of the century. At East Troy an old electric substation is part of the museum and the car-barn is just a block away. Adjacent to the museum is J. Lauber's Ice Cream Parlor, where one can order traditional ice cream sodas.

INFORMATION BOX

Termini	Milwaukee and East Troy, Wisconsin
Country	USA
Distance	8 km (5 miles)
Date of opening	1907

BOONE SCENIC RAILROAD

Iowa, located in the central portion of the United States, is largely an agricultural state. Near the centre of Iowa is Boone, once an important railroad town on the Chicago & North Western's busy main line between Chicago, Illinois, and Council Bluffs, Iowa. This was once a crew change and an important freight switching yard. Sadly there has been no regular passenger-service on this important main line in many years.

Amtrak crosses Iowa on the old Chicago, Burlington & Quincy (now operated by Burlington Northern Santa Fe) many miles to the south. A few miles west of Boone is the gigantic Kate Shelley High Bridge – named after a young woman who risked her life to warn a train of a washed-out bridge – which spans the valley of the Des Moines River. Today the Kate Shelley bridge handles 40–60 daily freight-trains operated by the Union Pacific Railroad (UP acquired the Chicago & North Western in 1995).

On the west side of Boone is the Boone & Scenic Valley Railway, a popular tourist line that operates steam, diesel and electric trains seasonally along the

● **ABOVE**
Every morning before it hauls passengers, Boone & Scenic Valley's steam-engine runs light (without cars) to the tall trestle in order to blow down its boiler – a procedure intended to remove mineral impurities.

● **LEFT**
Charles City & Western interurban car No. 50 is reminiscent of the sort of electric equipment that once ran on the Fort Dodge, Des Moines & Southern through Boone. The Boone & Scenic Valley runs the vintage electric at weekends in the summer.

● **OPPOSITE**
Boone & Scenic valley's Mikado takes on water between runs on a hot June day. Boone is proud of its railroad heritage and every year hosts "Pufferbilly Days" in September.

● **ABOVE LEFT**
Boone & Scenic Valley's Chinese-built 2-8-2 Mikado type marches into Boone, Iowa.

● **ABOVE RIGHT**
An eastbound Union Pacific coal-train crosses the Kate Shelley High Bridge. Although the big bridge has two tracks, it can only support the weight of one train at a time.

INFORMATION BOX

Terminus	Boone
Country	USA
Distance	11 km (7 miles)
Date of opening	1906

right of way of the Fort Dodge, Des Moines & Southern, known as the Fort Dodge Line – the largest of the Iowa interurbans. Iowa was once criss-crossed by lightweight electric interurban lines that carried freight and passengers. While most of these lines have been abandoned, a few segments remain in place, primarily as freight operations. This particular line operated under wire until the mid-1950s, when it was converted to diesel operation. In later years it was taken over by the Chicago & North Western and operated as a freight-only branch line. Several years ago, Boone & Scenic Valley acquired the picturesque route from the

C&NW and began operating passenger excursions. Since that time, Boone Scenic has re-electrified a short section of its line into town and operates an interurban car reminiscent of those that traditionally operated here.

In the summer the main attraction is Boone's steam-train, hauled by the brightly painted Chinese 2-8-2 Mikado type locomotive No. JS8419. This locomotive was ordered new by the railroad from the Datong works in 1988, and it was delivered in 1989 for the specific purpose of hauling passengers. The steam-train operates along the right of way of the old interurban north-west out of Boone, along the bucolic valley of the Des Moines River. The engineering highlight of the trip is Boone Scenic's high bridge, a 48 m (156 ft) tall trestle, which crosses a creek that feeds into the Des Moines River. Trains cross the bridge very slowly to allow passengers to admire the view.

During the summer the railroad operates three steam trips at weekends and one round trip on weekdays. Diesel-powered trips are offered at other times. For an extra fare, passengers can ride in the elevated cupola of a traditional American caboose. The electric portion of the line is also generally operated during summer weekends.

LOS MOCHIS TO CHIHUAHUA
THE COPPER CANYON

● **BELOW**
Here we see the train to Chihuahua starting its journey to Los Mochis.

In 1961, with the opening of the newest transcontinental railway in North America, the tremendous spectacle of canyons deeper and longer than Arizona's Grand Canyon was made available to travellers. However, they could only see it by rail, for there were no roads and certainly no airfields amid the wild Sierra Madre mountains of Mexico.

The Chihuahua Pacifico Railway is a success. In its 36 years of existence, it has carried millions of passengers – many of them from overseas. It runs for 655 km (407 miles) from Los Mochis on Mexico's west coast tidewater to the city of Chihuahua, passing through 87 tunnels and across 36 bridges. At one stage, it has to negotiate a triple loop to gain altitude. The summit is attained at kilometre post 583, some 2,502 m (8,209 ft) above sea level, near the halt of Divisadero where the Barranca (meaning copper) Canyon divides from the almost equally awesome Ulrique Canyon.

Originally planned at the end of the last century as a freight route for Texas and central America to serve the deep-water Pacific ports of Mexico, the railway took some 60 years to complete. Only

● **BELOW**
Here we see the train to Chihuahua starting its journey to Los Mochis.

surveyors and missionaries had ever been to these remote canyons, populated by a tribe of Tarahumara Indians who lived in caves in the canyon walls. The Tarahumara retain their traditions, and are mostly unable to speak Spanish, although they have a school at Creel, a logging township on the railway where a few basic roads exist. Travellers by train may see some of the more venturesome Tarahumaras selling souvenirs at stalls

beside the tracks at Divisadero, where all trains stop for 20 minutes to allow passengers to enjoy the wonderful views.

Two passenger-trains run each way daily, providing what is reckoned by experts to be among the world's five top scenic train rides. They are usually well patronized, and both make early morning starts to provide a daylight ride over the full length of the line. Foreign visitors to Mexico are often in a majority in the first

INFORMATION BOX	
THE COPPER CANYON	
Termini	Los Mochis and Chihuahua
Country	Mexico
Distance	655 km (407 miles)
Date of opening	1961

● **LEFT**
The arrival, from the Pacific, of El Tarahumara at Divisadero station. The train is named after the indigenous people of the canyons.

class, where meals are served. There are also freight services, usually one by day and one by night, serving the deep-water port of Topolobampo, some 20 km (12½ miles) beyond the growing city of Los Mochis.

Once a week, a set of special cars called the Sierra Madre Express are attached to the Mexican trains coming down from Nogales and are coupled to the first Chihuahua-Pacifico train over the Copper Canyon line. This takes place

at Sufragio, the junction of the new line with the Ferrocarril Pacifico. Usually two sleepers, a lounge, restaurant and dome car (all restored from US equipment of the 1950s) constitute the Sierra Madre Express, all of which make a very heavy load to haul up from sea level to 2,500 m (8,000 ft). Detached at Divisadero, these American cars lay over in the sidings, passengers sleeping aboard. They will have begun their "train cruise" in Arizona, and the special fares are high.

● **TOP LEFT**
The Rio Chinipas bridge is the highest on the line.

● **TOP RIGHT**
A parked US cruise train at Divisadero station.

● **ABOVE RIGHT**
Trains at Divisadero, Copper Canyon. On the left is the lounge car Arizona, which is part of the Sierra Madre train.

● **RIGHT**
The Copper Canyon. This is one and a half times deeper and longer than Colorado's Grand Canyon.

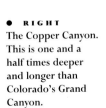

SANTOS TO SÃO PAULO

The São Paulo Railway in Brazil was described as Britain's most successful transportation investment abroad. Incorporated in 1856 as the San (this was a wrong interpretation, which the company retained all its working life) Paulo Railway, it was built to link the port of Santos with the healthy uplands of Brazil, mainly – in early days – for the coffee growers. It contributed greatly to the growth of São Paulo, now one of the biggest cities in the world and one of South America's most industrialized urban areas.

This unique line is a 5 ft 3 in gauge railway that is literally hoisted up the Serra do Mar, a mountain precipice, by an endless rope. It was always a full-scale main line with excellent rolling stock, first-class steam locomotives, restaurant cars and an efficient working practice. The whole journey was only 80 km (50 miles) in length, 19 km (12 miles)

through swamps at the coastal end and 53 km (33 miles) along a plain at the top, with 8 km (5 miles) of steep rope haulage in between. The best trains took just two hours for the journey, including up to 45 minutes "on the rope" if more than six coaches had to be hoisted (these were done three at a time). When diesel units were introduced after World War II, times were cut since the whole unit could

be hoisted in one go. The 99-year lease ran out in 1955, when the name of the railway, now under Brazilian ownership, was changed to Estrada de Ferro Santos a Jundia. The railway had been profitable from the start and the take-over was cordial, with huge amounts paid to shareholders at the end. But since then circumstances have changed, with the construction of a Canadian-financed

● **ABOVE**
Santos railway station where the journey begins.

● **LEFT**
One of the 0-4-0 tram-like steam brake-vans on the Santos a Jundia section of the line. As can be seen the engines produce a lot of smoke, so much so that they sometimes appear to be on fire.

● **RIGHT**
The journey starts at the beautiful seaside resort of Santos. Travellers must often be loath to leave the sandy beach.

● **BELOW LEFT**
São Paulo's Estación de la Luz (Station of Light). This 1936 scene shows the train to Santos about to depart. The locomotive would run the first 53 km (33 miles) to the start of the incline.

● **BELOW RIGHT**
Three coaches of a Santos-São Paulo train going up an incline with a breaking locomotive attached.

highway, the Anchieta, which sweeps up the escarpment to São Paulo, and on which cars and buses make the trip in under 90 minutes. There are now only two passenger-trains each way daily, all second-class, taking 115 minutes. They are still patronized because the fare is low compared to the buses. The ownership is now with Rede Ferroviaria Federal, São Paulo, a government department. After 1927, five new inclined planes were built on a gentler gradient (about 1:11), which speeded ascent and descent. Ropes are renewed every two years and re-spliced every six months. A trained gang re-splices a rope in 40 minutes. None has ever broken. The height above sea level at the top of the incline is 792 m (2,598 ft). The beautiful roofed Estación de la Luz (Station of Light) in São Paulo is still there as a reminder of the days of great prosperity and 12 per cent dividends.

INFORMATION BOX

SAN PAULO RAILWAY

Termini	Santos and São Paulo
Country	Brazil
Distance	80 km (50 miles)
Date of opening	1856

SANTA ROSA DE LOS ANDES TO LAS CUEVAS, ARGENTINA

● **BELOW**
A veteran steam branch-line train between
Loncoche Junction and Villarica in the Chilean
Lake District.

Although the Trans-Andine railway was
projected in 1854, work did not begin
until 1887, and the line was not finally
opened until 1910. Built to provide a rail
link over the Andes between Chile and
Argentina, the line now terminates at the
border between the two countries.

The first section of this metre-gauge
line, which goes 34 km (21 miles) from
Santa Rosa de Los Andes to Rio Blanco,
rises some 640 m (2,100 ft). On this
stretch the trains average about 29 kph
(18 mph). The second section of the trip,
from Rio Blanco to the frontier, about
two-fifths of the way through the
3,028 m (9,934 ft) long Uspallata tunnel,
is just under 36.5 km (23 miles) long and
rises 1,730 m (5,676 ft). In this 71 km
(44 mile) stretch of line, there are six
rack sections and no less than 26 tunnels
with a total length of 3,183 m (10,443
ft) – not counting the Uspallata. The
electric trains average about 18 kph (11
mph) on this stretch. The Uspallata

INFORMATION BOX

Termini	Santa Rosa de Los Andes and Las Cuevas
Countries	Chile and Argentina
Distance	71 km (44 miles)
Date of opening	1910

tunnel, between the peaks of the 7,040
m (23,097 ft) Aconcagua and the 6,187
m (20,298 ft) Tupungato , lies at an
altitude of 3,200 m (10,500 ft).

One of the locomotives used on the
line was a Shay type, built by Lima in
1904. It was carried on two four-
wheeled bogies with the tender on
another four-wheeled bogie. This engine
took light trains up the rack grades and

● **LEFT**
A view of the Paso
de los Liberadores
(the Pass of the
Freedom Fighters)
in the Andes on the
Chilean/Argentinean
border.

worked the section between Portillo and the Summit tunnel. There were also two 2-6-2T rack and adhesion engines, made by Borsig of Berlin. A 0-8-0+0-6-0T Meyer is kept at Los Andes mainly for use in snow clearance.

The main problems encountered on the route were, in winter, snow, which can reach as much as 6.4 m (21 ft) deep, and, in summer, rock falls and avalanches. Indeed, owing to the many landslides that have occurred over the years, the rail route over the Andes has now been closed for good – there is neither money nor incentive to restore it, especially as a road now crosses its path and, ironically, uses the rail tunnel beneath the great statue of Christ.

When the Trans-Andine train did run, it was at Las Cuevas, 3 km (2 miles)

into Argentina, that the Chilean crew with their Swiss-built Brown-Boveri electric locomotive would hand over the train to their Argentine colleagues with their Czech-built cog-wheel diesel unit. Once the start of a 1,088 km (676 mile)

journey to Argentina's Santiago Alameda station, the line is now mainly only used during the winter sports season, when the resort of Portillo, altitude 2,743 m (9,000 ft), suddenly comes to life with the influx of winter sports enthusiasts.

● **ABOVE LEFT**
A spacious Chilean State Railways restaurant car.

● **ABOVE RIGHT**
A main-line express, the "Trans-Andino Combinación" near Llay Llay, en route to Los Andes.

● **LEFT**
The Laguna del Inca (Inca Lake), which is seen as the train progresses on its journey.

● **LEFT**
A Swedish-built electric locomotive shunts coaches for the "Trans-Andino Combinación" at Llay Llay.

ASUNCIÓN TO ENCARNACIÓN

It has truly been said that a Paraguayan train journey is one of the most high-rated rail experiences in the world. Although Paraguay has other railways, only one, the Ferrocarril Presidente Carlos Antonio López, carries passengers. One of the abiding memories of a trip on the line is the firework display that comes from its fleet of 100 per cent wood-burning locomotives. This is a truly unforgettable experience.

The first section of the line, from Asunción to Paruguar, was opened in 1861. In 1889 it was acquired by the London-based, British-controlled Paraguay Central Railway. The line, which reached Encarnación in 1911, was nationalized in 1961. Originally built to the 5 ft 6 in gauge, in 1911 it was reduced so that it could be connected to

● **RIGHT**
One of the North British-built wood burners surrounded by wood at Colonel Belgrado.

● **BELOW**
A steam tram built by Borsig of Berlin for working around the docks of Buenos Aires. After a long life in the Argentinian capital, this veteran was pensioned off to the sugar fields of neighbouring Paraguay, and during its workaday chores it regularly sallies forth on to the international main line linking Asunción to Encarnación.

Argentina's standard gauge. Although the railway is run down and the line in poor condition, a trip over the line should be very high on the list of any South American traveller.

The 376 km (234 mile) journey, which lasts from 14 to 18 hours, commences at Asunción's multi-colonnaded colonial-style station and heads in a south-easterly direction across undulating countryside to Villarica. Thereafter the landscape changes to flat pampas and swampland for the rest of the journey to Encarnación. Here the through train to Argentina leaves the station to proceed down the length of a street towards the ferry terminal at Paca Cua. The coaches are then lowered on to

the train ferry by a steam-operated winch and cable. The ferry, which can carry six coaches at a time, crosses the Parana· River to Posadas, Argentina.

The twice-weekly train is usually hauled by one of the country's British-built locomotives, from the North British of Glasgow or the Yorkshire Engineering Company's Meadow Hall works in Sheffield. There are still Edwardian 2-6-0s in service. This sole passenger line in the country, where passenger comfort is an unheard-of concept, is operated with only nine passenger-cars. There used to be a sleeping car, but it was withdrawn in 1972. The restaurant car, which used to be fitted to the train, has also been out of use for some years, so that during the journey food has to be purchased from itinerant vendors along the track.

The future of this unique railway is in doubt. The new road bridge over the Parana River at Encarnación now brings road and rail traffic directly from

Argentina, rendering the ferry defunct. At present, all services are suspended, ostensibly for track up-grading, and it is hoped that the railway will eventually work again. This must be open to question, however, as traffic has dwindled progressively over recent years. At present the locomotive fleet of vintage rolling stock remains intact, as it waits for a tomorrow that may never come.

INFORMATION BOX

Termini	Asunción and Encarnación
Country	Paraguay
Distance	376 km (234 miles)
Date of opening	1861

JULIACA TO CUZCO
THE HIGHEST RAILWAY IN THE WORLD

Crossing the Andes meant constructing the highest railway in the world. Because of its altitude, the Peruvian Central Railway presented civil engineers with major problems, for, in a confined space and short distances, they had to build railways over passes that exceeded Mont Blanc in altitude. The solutions they adopted were tight curves, zigzags and rack sections.

Operating the lines was also fraught with difficulties: steep gradients, lack of local sources of fuel, heavy wear and tear on locomotives and rolling stock, and frequent landslides and washouts. Even the change from steam to diesel was, initially, a step backwards, because diesel

INFORMATION BOX	
THE HIGHEST RAILWAY IN THE WORLD	
Termini	Juliaca and Cuzco
Country	Peru
Distance	339 km (211 miles)
Date of opening	1908

units were prone to power loss in the rare atmosphere, and there were cases of trains being unable to take the gradients.

The three lines of the the Southern Railway of Peru serve the *altiplano*, a

windswept plain 3,901 m (12,798 ft) above sea level. Of standard gauge, they run to Mollendo on the Peruvian coast through the country's second city, Arequipa, to the town of Juliaca on the altiplano. Here the line divides. A short section continues to Lake Titicaca and around its shores to the port of Puno, while a 339 km (211 mile) line from Juliaca runs north to Cuzco, the ancient Inca capital, crossing a summit of 4,314 m (14,153 ft) at La Raya.

A glance at the map of Peru shows that the route of the Central Railway forms a lop-sided T, with Lima at its base, running up to La Oroya at the junction of the cross-piece. The main line runs from

● **LEFT**
A Hunslet 2-8-0 No. 108 at an isolated mountain stop on the Huancayo to Huancavelica line.

Lima through La Oroya to Huancavelica, its terminal, on the right. To the left, a privately owned railway runs from La Oroya to Cerro de Pasco, site of Peru's copper mines. The Southern and Central Railway systems are unconnected.

The Central Railway is regarded as one of the wonders of the Americas, and the engineering of the route involved immense problems. The deep Rimac valley between Lima and La Oroya, the only feasible route to the central region of the country, narrows to a maximum width of about 198 m (650 ft). Within its limits, the engineers had to find a way of climbing nearly 3,960 m (12,992 ft) within a distance of less than 76 km (47 miles). The twists and turns that the railway needs to gain height have made the railway considerably longer at 117 km (73 miles).

To keep the gradient down to 1:23, the line has to utilize the whole width of the valley, crossing frequently from one side to the other. Even this would be impossible without the use of the famous zigzags to gain height. Between Chosica and Ticlio, the highest point of the line at 4,783 m (15,692 ft), there are six double and one single zigzags, 66 tunnels, including the 1,177 m (3,861 ft) long

Galera, and 59 bridges, including that over the Verrugas, which, at 175 m (574 ft) long, when built in 1890, was the third longest in the world.

Construction of the line, which began in 1870, presented problems in addition to the geographical ones. A mysterious disease killed off thousands of workers in 1877, and Peru went bankrupt, which effectively held up completion until 1929. The chief reason for the Central

Railway has been freight-carrying, particularly since 1897 when the La Oroya copper mine opened. However, the incredible journey still remains attainable to travellers. Except for those unfortunates who suffer from altitude-sickness and have to be given oxygen by the white-coated attendants on the train, all will marvel at the ingenuity of the men who built this railway amid some of the most rugged landscapes on earth.

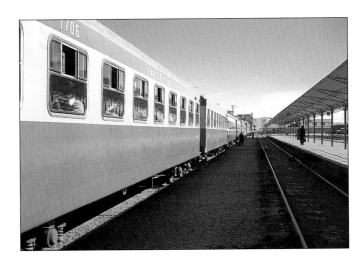

GUAYAQUIL TO QUITO

The chief component of the Ecuadorian State Railway is the Guayaquil to Quito line (misleadingly nicknamed the "Good and the Quick"), which connects the two major cities of the country; the former on the coast, the latter high up in the Andian mountains.

Construction work began in 1871, but it was not until 1908 that the contractors completed the rare 3 ft 6 in gauge line. To traverse the 463 km (288 miles) and 3,609 m (11,840 ft) altitude, tight curves and zigzags were incorporated. It has never been a commercial success and its resulting

● **LEFT**
Passengers board a first-class train on the Ibarra to San Lorenzo line.

● **LEFT**
Travellers on the *tren mixto* (mixed train) ready to leave Sibambe.

INFORMATION BOX

Termini	Guayaquil and Quito
Country	Ecuador
Distance	463 km (288 miles)
Date of opening	1908

● **BELOW**
A small Baldwin 2-6-0 No. 7 passes through Milagro non-stop on market day.

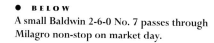

near-bankruptcy has given it a poor reputation for chaotic administration, breakdowns and derailments. Its lines are antique, and the fact that the railway is continuing to operate tends to raise more amazement than the fact that it was ever built. But for anyone interested in travelling on impossible railway lines, who is not put off by an uncomfortable ride punctuated by possible disasters, the G&Q must be a prized experience. It has sometimes been called "the world's mightiest roller coaster".

Guayaquil, Ecuador's second city, has its railway station at Duran, a long way out of town and on the opposite side of the Gyayas River estuary. The spectacular line to Quito begins its zigzagging course within a narrow gorge before climbing the famous Mariz del Diablo (Devil's Nose), a perpendicular ridge rising to a height of 3,230 m (10,597 ft). Another engineering challenge, this almost insurmountable obstacle was finally conquered by the construction of a series of switchbacks on a 5½ per cent grade. First one way and then the other, the train zigzags higher and higher to gain an altitude of 3,609 m (11,840 ft) at Urbino, a small town lying near the foot of the 6,705 m (21,997 ft) volcano of Chimborazo.

The northbound line from Quito runs to San Lorenzo on the coast. At least the line does, if not many services use it. It is erratic, to say the least, and a bus – sometimes – now takes over from the trains if the passenger load warrants it or if there's not enough freight for a *tren mixto*. Even today the *Thomas Cook Overseas Timetable* finds itself unable to prise proper timings of the service out of the administration.

The train, when it decides to put in an appearance, is a little monster called an *autocarril*. Basically this is a vehicle that was born as a British Leyland lorry and ended its life on flanged wheels and a fixed course. Although the ticket stipulates a reserved seat, there are in fact no seats to reserve.

On one occasion the River Mira cut the line in two by sweeping away the bridge. This meant that for a while the passengers had to alight and cross the river on a temporary rope structure, four at a time. A few kilometres on, along ill-laid and worn track, the train comes to a waterfall that descends directly on to the track to drench passengers who have failed to close their windows.

The total curvature of this line is no less than 16,200 degrees – the equivalent of more than 45 complete circles. The entire line is adhesion-worked and accounts for no less than 40 per cent of the country's total rail length.

● **ABOVE**
Looking down Devil's Nose as the train enters Sibambe.

● **LEFT**
A large Baldwin 2-8-0 No. 44 leaves Bucay on a *tren mixto* (mixed train), which has plenty of room on top.

DUBLIN TO CORK

The principal railway route in the Republic of Ireland is that which joins the country's two main cities, Dublin and Cork. It was built by the Great Southern & Western Railway and, like so many of the major trunk lines in the British Isles, it was a product of the railway mania of the 1840s.

Even by the standards of the time, the project was an ambitious one. At 265 km (165 miles), this line was longer than any comparable scheme in Britain. Given the much less favourable economic conditions in Ireland at the time – construction of the route was undertaken during the dark years of the Great Famine – the fact that the line was completed on schedule was a remarkable achievement. The line opened to a temporary station on the outskirts of Cork in October 1849, five years after the passing of the Act of Parliament authorizing the railway.

INFORMATION BOX

Termini	Dublin and Cork
Country	Ireland
Distance	265 km (165 miles)
Date of opening	1849

● **ABOVE**
The Dublin to Cork express speeds its passengers between two of Ireland's largest cities.

● **ABOVE LEFT**
The CIE logo used from the 1960s.

● **LEFT**
The train leaves the town and heads out into the beautiful Irish countryside.

The line starts from Heuston
(formerly Kingsbridge) station in Dublin.
The magnificent building that fronts the
station, containing offices and the board
room used by the three organizations that
have run the line over the decades, was
designed by the architect Sancton Wood
and opened in 1844. This is in marked
contrast to the rather dingy train shed,
which lurks behind the frontage and,
rather pointedly, is not physically
connected to it.

The route is relatively level except for
short sharp gradients at either end.
Leaving Dublin, trains are soon speeding
across the Curragh of Kildare where
thoroughbreds can be seen exercising on
the gallops alongside the track. After
passing through Portarlington,
Ballybrophy and Thurles, trains reach
Limerick Junction where, until track
changes were made in 1967, every train
serving the station since its opening in
1848 had to reverse to get into its
platforms. Here the line from Limerick
to Rosslare crosses the Cork line on the
level, the only such occurrence that is
met in Ireland today.

At Mallow the route that serves
County Kerry branches off, and the
tracks for Cork cross the River
Blackwater on a viaduct that replaced the
original one, destroyed in the Troubles of
the 1920s – one of the few notable
engineering feats of the line.

● ABOVE
A remarkable survivor from the dawn of the
railway age in Ireland is preserved under cover
in Cork station. This is 2-2-2 locomotive
No. 36, built by Bury, Curtis & Kennedy in
Liverpool for the commencement of services
on the Dublin to Cork line in the 1840s. It
remained in service, covering about half a
million miles in its time, until 1875. It was not
scrapped but remained at Inchicore works in
Dublin until the 1950s, when it was renovated
and put on display in Cork.

Approaching Cork the line plunges
into one of the longest railway tunnels in
Ireland at over 1,189 m (3,901 ft) in
length. The tunnel virtually brings a train
to the platforms of Cork station. The stiff
gradient through the tunnel provided a
daunting start for Dublin-bound trains in
the days of steam. The line continues
through the curving platforms of the
station to the final terminus at Cobh.
Cobh was known as Queenstown, and
was once a stopping-point for the great
Atlantic liners; it was also the last port of
call for the ill-fated *Titanic* in 1912.

Now a frequent service of fast express
trains runs throughout the day. The trains
are powered by the latest General Motors
diesels, and they generally operate at
speeds approaching 160 kph (100 mph).
There is, however, a reminder of the
line's earliest days in the foyer of the
station at Cork in the form of a steam
locomotive No. 36. A 2-2-2. This train
was built by Bury, Curtis & Kennedy
Company in Manchester for the opening
of the line in the 1840s, and is a
remarkable survivor from the dawn of
the Railway Age in Ireland.

DROMOD TO BELTURBET

Ireland was sadly lacking in deposits of coal and iron ore, the raw materials that fuelled the Industrial Revolution in the 19th century. One place where both these elements could be found was at Arigna in County Roscommon. Though the surrounding districts in the county of Leitrim were thinly populated and consisted of poor boggy land often inundated by the area's many lakes and streams, the prospective mineral wealth of Arigna led to plans being made in the 1880s for a narrow-gauge railway to connect Belturbet, County Cavan, in the north to Dromod, on the main Dublin to Sligo railway, in the south. A branch was planned from Ballinamore, midway along the route, to Arigna.

Most journeys along the line began at Dromod, where the narrow-gauge station adjoined the main-line one. The mixed train consisting of a tail of wagons and a carriage with a veranda and open platform at either end – shades of the

● ABOVE
At Belturbet the C&L shared a platform and station with the standard-gauge Great Northern branch. Trains on Ireland's two gauges are seen in this April 1956 view.

● LEFT
This Cavan to Leitrim train is being hauled by a 0-4-4 tank complete with cow-catcher.

● OPPOSITE BOTTOM
The deplorable state into which the locomotives had been allowed to fall is graphically illustrated in this view of Ballinamore shed in March 1959, just before the line finally closed.

INFORMATION BOX

Termini	Dromod and Belturbet
Country	Ireland
Distance	53 km (33 miles)
Date of opening	1887

● **LEFT**
One of the locomotives transferred to the C&L from the Cork, Blackrock & Passage line, when this closed in the 1930s, is seen here at Ballyconnell.

● **BELOW**
The view from the train on the roadside tramway to Arigna, which religiously followed the undulations and curves of the road for most of the way.

Wild West – threaded north through an area of small lakes and boggy land, with sharp curves and stiff gradients impeding progress. At the main stations, passengers were left to drum their fingers as the engine rambled off to shunt the goods yard. After 26 km (16 miles) the line's hub and headquarters at Ballinamore was reached. Here the main line was met by the branch from Arigna. For much of its 23 km (14 miles), the line, always known as the tramway, ran alongside the public road. It criss-crossed the road on ungated level crossings and stopped at road side halts distinguished only by name boards poking out of the hedges, and at one point passed over Ireland's longest river, the Shannon, here little more than a mountain stream.

From Ballinamore, the main line turned east to Belturbet, where the 3 ft gauge shared a station with a branch of the Great Northern Railway. Just outside the station, another of the great rivers of Ireland, this time the Erne, was bridged by a fine stone viaduct.

In later years there was just one train conveying passengers on this section. The journey from Dromod took three hours for the distance of 53 km (33 miles). This was a line on which passengers

would not have wanted to be in a hurry!

It was the carriage of Arigna's poor-quality coal that kept the Cavan & Leitrim in business up to 1959. Taken over by the Great Southern railway in 1925, as other narrow-gauge lines in the Irish Free State closed from the 1930s to the 1950s, their locomotives were transferred to the Cavan & Leitrim to cope with the sometimes hectic coal traffic. By the end, it was a veritable working museum and attracted rail fans from far and wide.

The memory of the gallant little line survived undimmed, and in the 1990s a new Cavan & Leitrim Railway Company was formed. Based at the southern terminus at Dromod, preservationists have re-laid part of the track and ultimately hope to run trains some 8 km (5 miles) to the next town of Molhill. This recreation of the railway, which has already brought the sight of a working 3 ft gauge locomotive back to County Leitrim, will rely on tourists and railway enthusiasts, not coal, for its revenues.

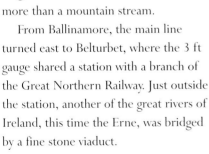

LONDONDERRY TO BURTONPORT

At its peak in the 1920s there were over 800 km (500 miles) of narrow-gauge railway open for service to the public in Ireland. The epic of these 3 ft gauge lines was the run from Derry to Burtonport on the tracks of the Londonderry & Lough Swilly Railway Company (L&LSR) in north-west Donegal.

The L&LSR began life as a standard-gauge line but converted its existing route from Derry to Buncrana to 3 ft gauge when a new narrow-gauge line from Derry to Letterkenny was opened in 1883. At this time the British Government was engaged in a policy of attempting to open up some of the more impoverished and remote districts in the west of Ireland by subsidizing the construction of railways in areas where they were of doubtful commercial viability. This was seen by some cynics as an effort to kill with kindness the agitation for Home Rule in Ireland.

Whatever the political motivation, it is hard to believe that serious investors could have been persuaded to put up the money for the extension of the L&LSR's Letterkenny line, which was promoted in 1898. It was to run through some of the

bleakest and poorest land in all of Ireland, and to terminate at the fishing harbour of Burtonport on the west coast of County Donegal. A separate company, the Letterkenny & Burtonport Extension railway, was formed to build the 80 km (50 mile) link, which opened in 1903 at

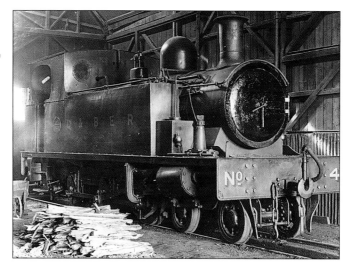

● LEFT
The line from Burtonport was built and, in theory at least, worked by a separate company, the Letterkenny & Burtonport Extension Railway. This was an attempt by the government to distance its enormous investment in the line from the other activities of the L&LSR. Among the first loco-motives acquired for the new line were a quartet of 4-6-0 tanks. No. 4, seen here in Londonderry, retained the initials of the L&BER to the end.

● ABOVE
The final engines supplied to the L&LSR were also unique and magnificent machines. Nos. 5 and 6 were 4-8-4 tanks built by Hudswell Clarke of Leeds, the only locomotives of this configuration to run on any gauge in the British Isles. They weighed 51 tons and had a tractive effort greater than many standard-gauge engines in use in Ireland at the time of their introduction in 1912.

● LEFT
4-6-0T No. 3 arriving at Letterkenny with a goods train from Derry, June 1950. The buses shown in the photo were operated by the L&LSR and continued in service decades after the trains ceased to run.

INFORMATION BOX	
Termini	Londonderry and Burtonport
Country	Ireland
Distance	119 km (74 miles)
Date of opening	1883

● RIGHT
4-8-0 No. 12 waits to head a train back to
Derry from Burtonport in June 1937. The
bleak rocky landscape seen in the picture is
typical of the area served by the line.

a cost to the public purse of some
£300,000. The line avoided most of the
tiny habitations it was supposed to serve
– allegedly to enable locals to find some
employment in ferrying goods and
passengers from these villages to their
distant stations.

The 119 km (74 mile) journey from
Londonderry to Burtonport took around
five hours in carriages that were unheated
in winter. It had been a difficult line to
construct, with whole sections of the
formation sinking into the boggy ground
before the track could be laid. Its main
engineering feature was the 347 m
(1,138 ft) long Owencarrow viaduct,
which was so exposed to gales howling in
from the Atlantic that in both 1906 and
1925 trains were blown off it. The 1925
accident resulted in the deaths of four
passengers. To work the line, two 4-8-0
tender engines were supplied by
Hudswell Clarke in 1905, by far the
largest narrow-gauge locomotives ever to
run in Ireland, and the only machines of
this type ever to operate in the British
Isles on any gauge.

The partition of Ireland severely
affected the fortunes of the L&LSR. The
city of Derry was in Northern Ireland,
while its natural economic hinterland in
County Donegal was now across an
international boundary in another
country. Fuel shortages occasioned by
World War II postponed the inevitable
for a few years, but the line beyond
Letterkenny finally closed completely in
1947, ending this heroic chapter in the
history of Ireland's minor railway.

● ABOVE
The Burtonport line soon spawned the largest locomotives ever to run on the
narrow gauge in the British Isles. Nos. 11 and 12 were 4-8-0 tender engines,
introduced in 1905, which looked more like the sort of engines found in India or in
southern Africa. No. 12 is seen near Derry with a Burtonport train in the 1920s.

● RIGHT
The line to Letterkenny and Burtonport left
the Derry to Buncrana at Tooban Junction,
an isolated spot near the shores of Lough
Swilly. 4-6-2 tank No. 10 is seen at the
junction on a special train in June 1953.

LEICESTER TO LOUGHBOROUGH

In May 1840 the Midland Counties Railway came to Leicester. On the fourth of the month, crowds were assembled at the town's new Campbell Street station as four first- and six second-class carriages, hauled by Leopard, arrived from Nottingham. After a short stop for the officials of the railway who lived in Leicester to take their places, the train pulled out of the station *en route* to Derby, where they dined at the King's Head before returning to Leicester.

The next day the station and all the surrounding area was crowded with spectators to witness the public opening. In spite of the cold, more and more people were arriving as the time of departure of the first train drew near. At seven-thirty the train, with its 50 passengers for Nottingham and Derby, started on its epic journey, reaching Syston, a distance of 9.5 km (6 miles), in 12 minutes.

The train reached Loughborough at eight o'clock where, once again, vast crowds were waiting to see the train, which arrived in Nottingham at nine o'clock. The following week the line was

- **LEFT**
The statue of Thomas Cook, the father of tourism, outside Leicester's London Road station. The work was commissioned by Leicester City Council in 1992 to mark the centenary of Cook's death.

- **BELOW**
Thomas Cook's grave in Leicester's Welford Road Cemetery.

- **RIGHT**
Built in 1894, two years after Thomas Cook's death, this terracotta building, Franco-Flemish in style, was the firm's Leicester office. At second-floor level, on four bronzed relief panels, are depicted four of the major events in Cook's career.

- **BELOW RIGHT**
The first of the panels shows the train involved in the 1841 excursion. Note that the passengers are travelling in what were affectionately known as "tubs".

- **LEFT**
The entrance to Campbell Street station, Leicester, as it appeared in December 1843 to mark the arrival of Queen Victoria. The station, built in 1841, was replaced by the present London Road station in 1892.

● **LEFT**
A view of
Loughborough
Midland station.

● **BELOW**
A Class 43 leaving
Loughborough on
the Midland Main
Line. It was on this
line that Thomas
Cook's historic first
railway excursion
took place.

INFORMATION BOX

Termini	Leicester and Loughborough
Country	England
Distance	16 km (10 miles)
First advertised rail excursion	5 July 1841

extended to Sheffield, a journey of 70 miles which took just over four hours.

In July 1841 Thomas Cook organized his first conducted tour. This was the first advertised excursion train in England – if not the world. With the co-operation of John Fox Bell, Secretary of the Midland Counties Railway, Cook arranged a special train to take people from Leicester to the quarterly temperance meeting at Loughborough. Bell not only agreed to the special train, but also gave Cook a contribution towards the preliminary expenses and agreed to a

half-price third-class fare of one shilling. On the morning of Monday 5 July, 570 people got into the nine open carriages, which had been provided for them. These carriages, called "tubs", were seatless open trucks in which the passengers stood unsheltered from the weather. As well as the crowds of people at Campbell Street station to witness the departure, all the bridges along the route

were lined with hundreds of people eagerly waiting for a look at the train.

Thus began, in the heart of the English Midlands, the company whose name has become synonymous with travel. By 1865 Cook's business had grown so big that he was organizing tours to the Continent and the USA and had had to relocate his head office from Leicester to London.

FORT WILLIAM TO MALLAIG

The start of this, arguably the most scenic rail journey in Britain, is Fort William, a town that nestles under the lofty peak of Ben Nevis. At 1,343 m (4,406 ft), this is Britain's highest mountain.

Soon after leaving the station, the train crosses the River Lochy, and then, at Banavie, the swing bridge over the 97 km (60 mile) long Caledonian Canal. Started by Thomas Telford in 1803, the canal traverses the Great Glen from Fort William to Inverness.

At Corpach, there is a pulp-paper mill, which is of note inasmuch as it is mainly responsible for the line remaining open. The West Highland line was used to deliver timber and then collect the finished product from the factory. After skirting the northern shore of Loch Eil, still with Ben Nevis in view, one soon arrives at Locheilside at the western end of the loch. This station, like others on the route, is still painted in the blue of the original Highland line. Having

● LEFT
The George Stephenson nameplate.

● BELOW
Locomotive No. 44767 George Stephenson crosses the Loch Eil causeway *en route* from Fort William to Mallaig.

● **LEFT**
An LNER locomotive on the West Highland line between Fort William and Mallaig.

● **BOTTOM**
The George Stephenson leaves Banavie with the 11.05 from Fort William to Mallaig.

travelled another 3 km (2 miles) through a narrow glen, the train reaches the Glenfinnan viaduct. It was near here that the Young Pretender, Bonnie Prince Charlie, unfurled his standard in 1745.

Built by Robert "Concrete Bob" MacAlpine, the 21 arches stand 30 m (100 ft) above the ground, the concrete structure curves in a crescent across the Finnan valley. During its construction a cart-horse and its driver were killed when the horse stumbled as it backed to tip its load into one of the shafts. The result was that cart, horse and driver were entombed in the wet concrete. A plaque recording the fatality can be seen on the viaduct.

After leaving Glenfinnan, the train travels through a wooded glen and emerge on the shores of Loch Eilt. From Lochailort station, there is a series of

short tunnels before a viaduct takes the train across Glen Mamie, after which it soon meets the Atlantic at Loch nan Uamh (Loch of the Cave). There are then a few more short tunnels before reaching Arisaig, from where the island of Eigg can be seen.

The line now turns north and at Morar crosses the River Morar. The river, which flows from Loch Morar, is 310 m (1,017 ft) deep, and as such the deepest

lake in Britain. Another 4.8 km (3 miles) brings the train to its destination, the small fishing port of Mallaig.

In the 1970s and 1980s, the pleasure of the journey was enhanced if the passenger, on payment of a supplementary fare, travelled in the observation saloon, where there was a running commentary on the various points of interest on the route. These wooden-bodied Gresley observation cars were the last two in service on British Rail. Although extremely popular, they were withdrawn when the turntable at Mallaig was dismantled, making it impossible for them to be turned. It is hoped that one of these coaches will be fully operational and running for the hundredth anniversary of the preserved Great Central Railway in Leicestershire in 1999. An added pleasure which is still available is that during the summer some of the trains are steam hauled.

INFORMATION BOX

Termini	Fort William and Mallaig
Country	Scotland
Distance	67 km (41³/₄ miles)
Date of opening	1901

EDINBURGH TO WICK/THURSO

Soon after leaving Edinburgh, the Forth and Clyde canal is crossed and the train eases slowly round a sharp right-handed curve to Larbert and Stirling, whose large station, still with semaphore signals, was built by the Caledonian Railway. The ground now becomes undulating, and there are distant mountains to be seen. Soon after leaving Stirling, the River Forth is crossed and an 8 km (5 mile) climb at 1:100 begins.

After leaving Perth, 111 km (69 miles) from Edinburgh, the most spectacular part of the run to Inverness begins. After the long climb to the summit of the line at Druimuachdar, 452 m (1,483 ft) above sea level, there is a lengthy undulating section through verdant farming country and woodland.

● LEFT
Named after Scotland's largest lake, Loch Lomond, locomotive No. 37412 speeds its passengers through the Scottish countryside *en route* to Inverness.

● BELOW
The Loch Lomond snakes its way past one of the lochs on its way to the Scottish Highland city of Inverness.

INFORMATION BOX

Termini	Edinburgh, Wick and Thurso
Country	Scotland
Distance	Wick 540 km (335 miles), Thurso 529 km (329 miles)
Date of opening	1871

Blair Atholl, approached over a castellated bridge, was important in the days of steam traction because banking locomotives were shedded at a small depot still visible to the left of the line. The 29 km (18 mile) length of the line, which raises the railway 315 m (1,033 ft) to the highest rail summit in the UK apart from Snowdon, imposed a great strain on locomotive crews and on the

steam-raising capacity of boilers. Even now, although the HST makes light of the climb, heavy trains hauled by diesel locomotives struggle in bad weather.

The Highland Railway originally reached Inverness down the Spey valley through the Boat of Garten, a junction with the Great North of Scotland Railway, and Grantown on Spey. This 97 km (60 mile) route was shortened by 42 km (26 miles) by constructing a line from Aviemore through what was then wild country over the Slochd Pass, 401 m (1,315 ft) above sea level.

The train leaves Inverness round a left-handed curve and soon crosses the river Ness on a bridge replaced fairly recently after the original collapsed in severe flooding. A spirited run along the Beauly Firth provides fine views to the right before the train swings away from the water through the Muir of Ord to Dingwall. The line now heads north-west, following the coastal plain before swinging north-east to Tain on the picturesque Dornoch Firth, where it starts to climb alongside the Kyles of Sutherland to Culrain.

There follows a sharp climb at 1:70/72 as the line passes through a rocky gorge and past the small town of Lairg on its way to a summit 149 m (489 ft) above sea level, after which it swings east and drops down through pleasant scenery past the small Loch Fleet to reach the coast again at Golspie. A little further on is Dunrobin Castle, the seat of the Dukes of

Sutherland, which had its own private railway station and a shed to house the duke's own locomotive and carriage.

The railway follows the coast for another 24 km (15 miles) and, after Helmsdale, begins to climb again, in places as steeply as 1:60, toward the bleak but impressive uplands. At Forsinard, where a small group of houses and some trees cluster around the station building, the railway parts company with

the track, which goes straight on down Strath Halladale. The line swings sharply east, rising to 216 m (709 ft) at County Marsh summit, after which it descends until, 6.4 km (4 miles) further on, it is a surprise to come upon a station, Altanbreac. It then continues down to the wide coastal plain and the rail junction of Georgemas, where trains were divided, one section going to Wick and the other to Thurso.

● **ABOVE LEFT**
This small shop proclaims itself to be the first and last on mainland Britain. The house built by Jan de Groot (corrupted to John o' Groat) is nearby.

● **ABOVE RIGHT**
The striking blue of the erstwhile Caledonian Railway adorns No. 828, once belonging to that railway, as it waits at the Boat of Garten to take its train to Aviemore on the main line to Inverness.

● **LEFT**
A view from the castle of Edinburgh's world-famous Princes Street. The park between the castle and the street is on the site of a long dried-up loch.

SETTLE TO CARLISLE

The Settle to Carlisle line, which transports the traveller from the Yorkshire Dales through the desolate mountain scenery of the north-west, is one of the most scenic in England. For most of the journey, which takes in 14 tunnels and 19 viaducts, the line runs at an altitude of over 305 m (1,000 ft). One of the tunnels, the 137 m (450 ft) deep Blea Moor tunnel, is a massive 2,404 m (7,887 ft) long.

The Yorkshire village of Settle, where the journey starts, lies about 137 m (450 ft) above sea level. Although work began on the line in 1869, it was not until 1876 that the first passengers were able to enjoy the stupendous views that the line commands. The building of the line was not without incident, as can be seen from the plaque in the village church. Erected by the Midland Railway, it commemorates the men who lost their

● **LEFT**
No. 4498 Sir Nigel Gresley leaves Rise Hill tunnel on the approach to Dent station.

● **BELOW LEFT**
The West Yorkshire Dalesman, hauled by locomotive No. 5305, approaches the summit at Ais Gill Cottages *en route* to Carlisle.

lives while building the 27 km (17 miles) of track between Settle and Dent Head.

The first 21 km (13 miles) of the line travels through the Ribble valley to an elevation of 320 m (1,050 ft). After 18 km (11 miles) the train crosses the Ribblehead viaduct. Built out of limestone and red brick between 1870 and 1874, at 32 m (105 ft) high this handsome viaduct is one of the highlights of the journey. The remoteness of the

INFORMATION BOX

Termini	Settle and Carlisle
Country	England
Distance	115 km (71 miles)
Date of opening	1876

● **LEFT**
The Ribblehead viaduct, built between 1870 and 1874 out of limestone and red brick. At 32 m (105 ft) high, this is one of the high points of the journey.

● **BELOW**
The Flying Scotsman heads the Cumbrian Mountain Express. It is seen here at Great Ormside heading south *en route* from Appleby to Hellifield.

line can be gauged from the fact that Blea Moor signal box stands some 1.2 km (³/₄ mile) from the nearest road, and that Dent station is 6.4 km (4 miles) and 213 m (700 ft) above the village it serves. In winter the weather can be worse than anywhere else in England, with prolonged bouts of heavy snow. To prevent the snow from drifting on to the line, fences have been erected in the exposed mountain areas.

From Appleby to Carlisle the train passes through the Vale of Eden. Never encountering gradients of over 1:100, the line is laid some 15–30 m (50–100 ft) above river level. This makes it less liable to flooding, an important factor as the annual precipitation in this area can be over 2.5 m (100 in) per year.

The end of the journey is Carlisle station, which, in the early part of the century, with many railway companies jointly using it, was bustling with activity. Once an important artery between the city of Leeds and the north-west, the line is now one of the country's foremost lines for seeing, and travelling by, preserved steam locomotives.

The Settle and Carlisle is one of the finest preserved lines in Britain. A journey on these tracks is a trip back in time that every rail enthusiast should experience at least once in their lifetime.

LONDON EUSTON TO GLASGOW

This is one of the most historic lines in Britain, including, as it does, major lengths of Robert Stephenson's London & Birmingham and Joseph Locke's Grand Junction Railway. Although the title of Royal Scot was not bestowed until 1927, the train that bore the name was one of the oldest established in Britain, having first pulled out of Euston for Glasgow in June 1862. Up until 1914 the train left London Euston at 10.00, stopping at Willesden Junction, Rugby, Crewe (where it divided, with one section going on to Edinburgh) and Symington, reaching Glasgow eight and a quarter hours later.

In the summer of 1927, the LMSR made the Royal Scot a train for through passengers between London, Glasgow and Edinburgh only. The double-headed train, hauled by a Claughton 4-6-0 and a George the Fifth 4-4-0, stopped only twice – once at Carnforth, 380 km (236 miles) from Euston, where two 4-4-0

compounds took over for the run over Shap and Beattock summits to the second stop, Symington, 209 km (130 miles) further on, where the Edinburgh part of the train was detached. In 1928, hauled by Royal Scot 4-6-0 No. 6113 Cameronian, the Glasgow train made a non-stop run of

645.8 km (401.3 miles), a British record for any type of locomotive.

The most scenic part of the journey is the stretch north of Wigan, which starts with a sharp climb of about 3 km (2 miles) at 1:104, and then one at 1:119 to the summit of Coppull. Although the

● **ABOVE**
A southbound Birmingham to Euston train leaves Proof House Junction, south of Birmingham's New Street Station.

● **LEFT**
A scene at Wolverhampton's No. 1 Lock as a Euston to Glasgow InterCity train, hauled by a Class 86 electric locomotive, enters the station.

● **RIGHT**
A Euston-bound
train near
Ecclefechan,
Galloway, on the
first part of the
journey.

● **RIGHT**
A Euston-bound
train near
Ecclefechan,
Galloway, on the
first part of the
journey.

● **BELOW LEFT**
A southbound
Glasgow to Euston
train beside the M1 in
Northamptonshire.

● **BELOW RIGHT**
An RES (Rail Express
Systems) liveried
Class 86 heads
southwards through
Cumbria on the West
Coast main line.

next section of the track was conducive to high-speed running, speed restrictions were necessary owing to subsidence (erosion) caused by mine workings. At Boars Head the subsidence was so severe that the windows of the station waiting-room sunk to the level of the platform.

After the almost level track through the Lune Gorge comes one of the steepest main-line inclines in Britain – the 6.4 km (4 mile) long 1:75 climb to Shap summit, 279 m (915 ft) above sea level. From the summit there is a 51 km (32 mile) long run of unbroken downhill running to Carlisle.

Until the 1923 regrouping, Carlisle station was one of the most colourful in the British Isles, with many companies' locomotives in their bright liveries to be seen. These included the crimson of the Midland, the blue of the Caledonian, the bright green of the North Eastern and the yellow of the North British.

After crossing the into Scotland at Gretna, much of the ten tonnes of coal with which the train started off had been used and the "coal-pusher", a piston operated by steam that shoved the coal forward from the rear of the tender, was set to work. A sign that the coal-pusher was in action was a jet of steam trailing from the top of the tender.

Just beyond Wamphray began the most gruelling climb on any British main line. Although most trains had to take on rear-end assistance, the Royal Scot charged unaided up the formidable 16 km (10 mile) long 1:74 grade to Beattock Summit, 318 m (1,043 ft) above sea level.

From here the train descended into Glasgow Central station, which opened in 1879. Although remodelled some 12 years later, it was still found to be inadequate for the growing traffic, and in 1906 it underwent further changes, to more than double the station's capacity.

INFORMATION BOX

Termini	London, Euston and Glasgow, Central
Countries	England and Scotland
Distance	645 km (401 miles)
Date of opening	5 July 1841

LONDON KING'S CROSS TO EDINBURGH WAVERLEY
THE FLYING SCOTSMAN

The name Flying Scotsman entered railway language on 1 January 1923. When the first expresses from London to Edinburgh began in 1862, the journey took 10½ hours; today it takes 4 hours and 35 minutes. Up to 1935, Ivatt's Atlantics were usually at the head of the train between London and Leeds; an A3 Pacific between Leeds and Newcastle; and a Heaton Pacific between Newcastle and Edinburgh.

London's King's Cross station was designed by Lewis Cubitt and built by John Jay in 1852. Today this station is one of the smallest London termini with only eight main-line and two suburban platforms. As the train leaves King's Cross, it passes St Pancras train shed. Designed by W.H. Barlow, the 210 m (689 ft) long, 30 m (98 ft) high building has a glass and iron roof, which spans 74 m (243 ft). When this magnificent feat of engineering was built, it was the widest in the world.

After passing through nine tunnels, the train travels over the stately Welwyn viaduct. Designed by Lewis Cubitt, the structure contains 40 solid brick arches, which reach 27 m (89 ft) at their maximum height over the Mimram valley.

All the original GNR stations between King's Cross and Doncaster, such as Stevenage, Hitchin, Huntingdon and Peterborough, were built using local materials by the Leicester-born Henry Goddard. Shortly after leaving Peterborough, the train reaches the 24 km (15 mile) long Stoke Bank, the summit of which, 105 m (345 ft) above sea level, is the highest point reached by the train this side of the border.

Travelling north the gradient steepens from 1:440 to 1:178 until, at the top, the train enters the 805 m (2,640 ft) long Stoke Tunnel, after which it descends to the town of Grantham. This is the stretch of line on which, in July 1938, Gresley's Mallard reached the world steam record of 203 kph (126 mph).

There are several flat crossings on this part of the line. One of these, just before Retford, was the scene of an accident in which the driver of a down express saw a goods train ambling straight across his

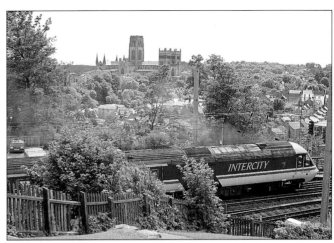

path. Having no time to brake, the quick-thinking driver accelerated and cut the goods train in two, thereby saving his train at the expense of only two or three goods wagons.

After leaving Doncaster, the train runs along a curving viaduct into Wakefield, before beginning its 3 km (2 mile) climb of 1:122 to Ardsley. Following a descent of 1:50 the train enters Leeds Central terminus, from which, after a short halt, the train retraces its steps for a short way before bearing right to strike up the 1:100 8 km (5 mile) long Headingley Bank. Just past the summit, the train plunges into Bramhope Tunnel. At 3.42 km (2 miles and 234 yd) long, Bramhope Tunnel is the seventh longest tunnel in the country. Beyond it, the gradient alters sharply to a downhill 1:94.

The train approaches Newcastle over the Tyne by the High Level Bridge. Designed by Robert Stephenson for both road and rail, this was the first major bridge-building work on which James Nasmyth's steam-driven pile-driver was used. Begun in April 1846, with a total weight of over 5,000 tons, this is the earliest example of a dual-purpose structure. The upper deck was for the railway, the lower for the road.

The next big bridge to be crossed is the 658 m (2,159 ft) long Royal Border Bridge, also built by Robert Stephenson, which was opened by Queen Victoria in 1850. Over 2,000 workers were engaged

● **ABOVE LEFT**
This picture clearly shows the two famous arches that are a feature of King's Cross station, London.

● **ABOVE RIGHT**
An InterCity train passes Durham Cathedral, the last resting-place of St Cuthbert.

● **BELOW**
350 miles to go until London.

INFORMATION BOX

THE FLYING SCOTSMAN

Termini	London King's Cross and Edinburgh, Waverley
Countries	England and Scotland
Distance	650 km (404 miles)
Date of opening	1 January 1923

in building the fine 28 redbrick semicircular arches, each with a span of 18.7 m (61 ft 4 in).

After crossing the border, the railway hugs the coastline as it ascends the 6.4 km (4 miles) of 1:190 up to Burnmouth. On passing Grantshouse the train enters the Penmanshiel tunnel. The line was closed temporarily in 1979 after a fall had killed two men who were working in the tunnel.

The train enters Waverley station through the Calton tunnel, opened in June 1846. Edinburgh's first station was confined to the narrow valley between the old and new towns of the city, and became congested. A new station, covering 23 acres, said to be the second biggest in Britain, was opened in 1900.

LONDON PADDINGTON TO SWANSEA – *THE RED DRAGON*

● **BELOW**
A Class 143 Regional Railways train outside Radyr, near Cardiff.

● **BELOW**
A Class 143 Regional Railways train outside Radyr, near Cardiff.

The Red Dragon service, between London Paddington and Swansea (Abertawe), was first run in the winter of 1950–51. Departing Swansea at 08.45, the train made stops at Cardiff (Caerdydd) and Newport (Casnewydd-ar-Wysg), before completing the final 214 km (133 miles) of the journey to Paddington, non-stop in 165 minutes, arriving at 13.05. The return trip was 30 minutes longer. Leaving Paddington at 17.55, it made additional stops at Swindon and Badminton, so that Swansea was not reached until 22.45.

Reading station was the first of Brunel's one-sided stations, and one of the last survivors. All that remains of the original is the building on the southernmost platform. It was here that one of the first accidents on the Great Western occurred. While the station was being built, Henry West, a carpenter, was fatally blown from the roof by a "whirlwind".

About 14 km (9 miles) from Reading the train crosses Basildon Bridge, which was built in 1839 and extended in the 1890s. Its four redbrick 19 m (62 ft)

INFORMATION BOX

THE RED DRAGON

Termini	London, Paddington and Swansea
Countries	England and Wales
Distance	307 km (191 miles)
Date of first run	1950

arches cross the Thames uniting Berkshire and Oxfordshire. The line soon returns to Berkshire by means of Moulsford Bridge.

At the western end of Steventon, 18 km (11 miles) further on, the line crosses "The Causeway". One mile long, this is a raised flood path lined with trees and 17th- and 18th-century houses. A further 16 km (10 miles) brings us to Uffington, famous for its "White Horse", which can be seen from the train. This is 114 m (374 ft) from nose to tail and is believed to have been first cut into the hillside about 100 BC. Although called a horse it is more than likely that it was meant to be a dragon, for nearby is Dragon Hill on which, so folklore tells us, St George slew the fabled beast.

Swindon station, 124 km (77 miles) from Paddington, was originally built in 1841–42. A feature of the station was the hotel and dining-room connected to it by a covered overbridge. The original agreement was that all trains passing through should have a ten-minute refreshment stop here. Swindon was the site of Brunel's Great Western works, which were completed in 1843. The last

● BELOW
A driver's-eye view from the cab of an
InterCity 125 as it approaches the up train on
the line between Paddington and Swansea.

● BELOW
The "Welcome to Wales" sign that greets
passengers as the train leaves the Welsh side
of the Severn tunnel.

steam engine built at the works was
Evening Star, which entered service in
May 1960.

Badminton station, 160 km (100
miles) from Paddington, was specially
built for the Duke of Beaufort, who
demanded that any train had to stop at
his request – until, that is, an Act of
Parliament put a stop to his right. It was
here that the eponymous game was first
played. A few miles out of Badminton,
the train goes under the Cotswold Hills
through the 406 m (1,332 ft) long
Chipping Sodbury tunnel.

First sketched out by Charles
Richardson in 1865, the Severn tunnel,
after twice being flooded out, was finally
completed in 1886 at the cost of nearly
£2 million (then $3.2 million).
Connecting Wales to England, at 4,064 m
(13,333 ft) long it is the largest main-line
railway tunnel in Britain. The tunnel

shortened the route from London to
South Wales by 40 km (25 miles). Before
then, popular belief held that GWR stood
for the "great way round".

Just before Newport the line crosses
the River Usk. The first bridge, one of
Brunel's wooden viaducts, was damaged
by fire during construction. Remarkable
as it sounds, out of the many wooden
viaducts built by Brunel, this was the only
one to suffer such a fate. It was later

rebuilt, but this time in wrought iron.

Cardiff Central station, 233 km (145
miles) from Paddington, was first built in
1850. To create a site for the station, the
River Taff had to be diverted. The station
was modernized in the 1920s. On leaving
the Welsh capital, the line turns inland
until it regains the coast near Margam,
after which it skirts Swansea Bay, passing
through Port Talbot and Neath before
arriving at Swansea.

● OPPOSITE
The English portal
of the Severn tunnel,
connecting Wales
and England.

● RIGHT
A scene near
Sonning Cutting.
Although passengers
in the train do not
get a good view of it,
Sonning Cutting is
an engineering
achievement at
18 m (60 ft) deep
and nearly 3 km
(2 miles) long. It was
built in the autumn
and winter of 1839
and opened in
March 1840.

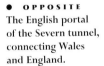

LONDON EUSTON TO HOLYHEAD
THE IRISH MAIL

The London & North Western Railway's Irish Mail was the world's first named train. Known unofficially as the "Wild Irishman", it departed from Euston station for the first time in August 1848. After passing through the 1,080 m (3,543 ft) long Primrose Hill tunnel, the train entered Acton Lane station (named Willesden Junction in 1866), which was built in 1842. Owing to its two groups of completely separate high-level platforms, and the fact that nobody knew at which platform any particular train was to arrive at or depart from, the station was unofficially nicknamed "Bewildering Junction" by its passengers.

Some 27 km (17 miles) into the journey the train passes through the Watford tunnel. 1.65 km (1 mile and 57 yd) long, the tunnel was built so that the railway line did not cross over the land of the Earl of Essex.

After another 56 km (35 miles) the train passes over the Wolverton viaduct. Over 200 m (660 ft) long with six arches, each with an 18 m (60 ft) span, the viaduct is at the centre of an

● LEFT
A 20th-century InterCity train passes the 13th-century Conwy Castle.

embankment 2.4 km (1½ miles) long and 15 m (49 ft) high. After a further 16 km (10 miles), Kilsby tunnel is reached. At 2,216 m (7,270 ft) in length, when it was built, at a cost of £290,000 (then $460,000), it was the longest railway tunnel in the world.

Passing Manchester, Crewe and Chester, the train then runs along the North Wales coast. After going through Rhyl and Colwyn Bay the line goes under the steep slope of the almost precipitous headland of Penmaen Mawr. As there was not enough room between the

mountain and the shore, in some places the rock had to be blasted and in others sea walls had to be built up to enable the line to be laid. A tunnel 211 m (693 ft) long was cut through the headland and, in some places, where the line ran close under the steep mountain face, covered ways were built as a precaution against falling stones.

During its construction, in October 1846, a north-westerly gale, combined with a spring tide of 5 m (16 ft), destroyed a large part of the work on the westward side of the headland. It was

● LEFT
An InterCity train on the London to Holyhead route.

● **LEFT**
The Brittania Bridge
built by Robert
Stephenson in 1850.

● **BELOW**
The Irish Mail.

then decided to cross the section by means of the big, curving, open viaduct that brings the train into Bangor. Work on the viaduct was eventually finished in 1849.

In the days of steam, in order to permit non-stop running between Chester and Holyhead, just before Bangor, near Aber, the speeding train would scoop up water from troughs laid between the tracks. Laid down in 1860, these were the world's first railway water troughs.

Next comes the Menai Strait tubular railway bridge leading to Anglesey. Built by Stephenson, the bridge spans 335 m (1,100 ft) of water near to Britannia Rock, from which it gets the name of Britannia Bridge. Stephenson's first plan

was to construct it out of cast iron. However, this was rejected by the Admiralty, who insisted that under no circumstances was the navigation of the Strait to be interrupted. After toying with various plans, in March 1845 Stephenson finally decided on the tubular wrought-iron beam with openings of 140 m (459 ft) and a roadway, formed of a hollow wrought-iron beam, about 6 m (20 ft) in diameter.

Built by a team of about 1,500 workers, the bridge has four spans, two of 140 m (460 ft) over the water and two of 70 m (230 ft) over the land. It was

opened for the public on 18 March 1850. Before the opening of the bridge, passengers had to disembark in Bangor and cross the Menai Strait by coach via Telford's suspension bridge.

The short run over Anglesey passes Llanfair PG, or, to give it its 58-letter name, coined by the local innkeeper in the 19th century, Llanfairpwllgwyngyllgogerychwyrndrobwllllantysiliogogogoch. Renowned for having the world's longest railway sign, the station was re-opened in 1973. Then the train soon reaches Holyhead – and the ferry that conveys passengers to Ireland, the Emerald Isle.

INFORMATION BOX

THE IRISH MAIL

Termini	London, Euston and Holyhead
Countries	England and Wales
Distance	425 km (264 miles)
Date of first run	1 August 1848

LONDON PADDINGTON TO PENZANCE

One of the most exciting and interesting rail journeys in England is that from London Paddington to Penzance, at the south-westerly tip of Cornwall. When the line opened, in August 1859, not only did almost all the trains stop at all stations, but passengers also had to change at Exeter and Plymouth. On arrival in Truro, a horse-drawn bus took them on to Falmouth, where the travellers boarded the West Cornwall narrow-gauge railway for the 33-minute ride to Penzance. The fastest time for the whole journey was some 14 hours and 50 minutes.

1862 saw the introduction of the Flying Dutchman, a train which did the journey from Paddington to Churston,

INFORMATION BOX

Termini	London and Penzance
Country	England
Distance	490 km (304 miles)
Date of opening	1859

on the Torquay branch of the South Devon Railway, at an average speed of 89.6 kph (56 mph), making it possible to reach Penzance in 10 hours and 19 minutes. The following year the line was extended from Truro to Falmouth,

● **BELOW**
Cornish Riviera Limited. The first train of this
name ran in 1904.

thereby making the equine transport
redundant. By 1867 the broad gauge was
extended to Penzance.

In 1890 the Great Western
introduced the Cornishman express,
which, by cutting out a number of
intermediate stations, was able to reach
Penzance in 8 hours and 42 minutes.
After the conversion from broad to
standard gauge in 1892, the Flying
Dutchman was able to cut a further 15
minutes off its time, so becoming the
fastest train in the world.

In 1896 the Cornishman posted a
time of 3 hours and 43 minutes for a

● **OPPOSITE ABOVE**
When the station was built Paddington was
still just a village. In the booking hall is a
diminutive statue of Isambard Kingdom
Brunel which was unveiled in May 1982.

● **OPPOSITE BELOW**
One of the few Brunel stations left, Dawlish
station, built in 1846, is lovingly preserved.
Here an InterCity train leaves the station *en
route* to Penzance.

● **ABOVE LEFT**
A section of the dramatic coastal track
between Dawlish and Teignmouth.

● **RIGHT**
An InterCity train crosses the Huntspil River at
the Somerset Levels. This is one of the wettest
areas in England with an average annual
rainfall of 101 cm (40 in). Much of the area is
below sea level and liable to periodic flooding.

● **LEFT**
The Penzance bound train passes through
Cockwood Harbour.

non-stop run to Exeter – then at 310 km
(194 miles) the longest non-stop route in
the world – cutting the time to Penzance
to 7 hours and 52 minutes.

In July 1904, by running non-stop to
Plymouth, the time was reduced even
more when the Limited express reached
Penzance in 7 hours dead. In May 1914,
the time was cut to 6½ hours and, in
1927, with the introduction of the King
Class, the most powerful engines in the
British Isles, the Cornish Riviera reduced
the time by a further five minutes to
6 hours and 25 minutes.

Soon after departing Paddington
Station, which was designed by Brunel
and opened in 1854, the train passes
over the 274 m (899 ft) long Wharncliffe
Viaduct. Built in 1838, the eight 21 m
(69 ft) brick spans tower 20 m (65 ft)
above the ground. The next point of
interest on the route is Sounding Arch
Bridge, which was built in 1838 and
widened in 1891. Considered to be one
of Brunel's finest bridges, it cost £37,000
(then $59,200) to build and consists of
two of the largest, flattest arches ever
built in brick, each with a span of 39 m
(128 ft) with a rise of only 7.4 m (24 ft
3 in). It is this bridge that is depicted in
Turner's painting, *Rain, Steam and Speed*.

Although passengers in the train do
not get a good view of it, Sonning

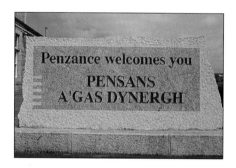

● **ABOVE**
On getting off the train, visitors to Penzance
are welcomed by this bilingual greeting in
both English and Cornish.

● **BELOW**
The holiday is over. The train to Paddington
leaves Penzance.

Cutting, 18 m (59 ft) deep and 6.5 km
(nearly two miles long), is another
remarkable achievement, built in 1839
and opened in March 1840. The
excavation was fraught with difficulties as
torrential rain flooded the area and
reduced the site to a quagmire.

One of the features of the line was
Brunel's celebrated one-sided stations.
With both platforms on the same side,
but a short distance apart, the design
obviated the necessity for passengers to
cross the line. Examples of these, now
totally rebuilt stations, which must have
caused chronic operating difficulties,
include Reading, Taunton and Exeter.

After the 998 m (3,274 ft) long
Whiteball Tunnel, which marks the
boundary of Somerset and Devon, there
is a flat coastal run, taking in the five
tunnels between Dawlish and Teignmouth
– Kennaway, Phillot, Clerk's, Coryton and
Parsons. In 1905 these tunnels were
widened to accommodate double tracks.

Newton Abbot was where Brunel set
up his atmospheric railway. The concept
of this was that, instead of being hauled
by steam engines, the carriages were

The 12.25 Great Western train from London to Bristol, showing the Great Western's new livery, at Swindon.

propelled by a vacuum caused by compressed air being pumped through a pipe between the rails.

Separating Devon and Cornwall is the 338 m (1,109 ft) long Royal Albert Bridge, which spans the River Tamar, the world's only chain-link suspension bridge to carry express trains. Widely regarded as Brunel's masterpiece, the two main tubular spans, each 137 m (450 ft) long and weighing over 1,077 tonnes (1,060 tons), are supported by three piers that allow a clearance of at least 30 m (100 ft)

above the water. The central underwater pier is anchored on hard rock 24 m (79 ft) below the high-water level and was built by masons working in a pressurized diving bell – the first such use in civil engineering. It took seven years to build and was opened by Prince Albert in May 1859, four months before Isambard Kingdom Brunel's death.

Over the 85 km (53 miles) between Plymouth and Truro, the train crossed 34 of Brunel's timber viaducts, now replaced by masonry ones. The viaducts,

which crossed the many deep and narrow valleys of the area, were constructed in two standard spans of 20 m (66 ft) for the Cornwall and Tavistock lines and 15 m (50 ft) for the West Cornwall structures.

The line reached Penzance in March 1852, when it opened to standard-gauge trains. Fifteen years later, in March 1867, the Great Western's broad gauge reached the town. The present station, which has a charming sign welcoming visitors in the now almost dead language of Cornish, was built about 1865.

● ABOVE RIGHT
The Mayflower entering Exeter St Davids station.

● LEFT
The train crossing the sea wall at Dawlish. The town of Dawlish is often the victim of fierce storms. One such, in 1974, washed away most of the down platform.

LONDON VICTORIA TO DOVER
THE GOLDEN ARROW

Although the Southern Railway (and its predecessor the South Eastern & Chatham Railway) had maintained a service from London Victoria to Paris, it was not until 15 May 1929 that the title Golden Arrow was bestowed upon the train. The first trains were hauled by 4-6-0 Lord Nelson Class and were exclusively for first-class Pullman passengers; however, two second-class cars were added in the 1940s. After World War II, the Lord Nelson Class was

The Golden Arrow travelling through Ashford, Kent.

The Golden Arrow coming into Headcorn station. This view is taken from Fritten Road Bridge.

replaced by Oliver Bulleid's Merchant Navy Class 4-6-2s. Bulleid, a New Zealander by birth, was the Chief Mechanical Engineer of the Southern Railway. Then, in 1951, Britannia 4-6-2 Standard Class 7s were introduced to the service. One of these, No. 70004, William Shakespeare, was exhibited at the 1951 Festival of Britain.

The Golden Arrow was one of the first trains in England to be fitted with a public address system, through which the international passengers were addressed in English and French.

Another feature of the train was the Trianon cocktail bar, reminiscent of a high-class club, where the rich were able to sup their way to the Continent. The exclusive first-class train lasted only two years, for by May 1931 the weight of the

INFORMATION BOX

THE GOLDEN ARROW

Termini	London Victoria and Dover
Country	England
Distance	113 km (70 miles)
Date of first run	15 May 1929

● **RIGHT**
The Golden Arrow
seen here between
Tonbridge and
Sevenoaks.

● **BELOW RIGHT**
King Arthur Class
4-6-0 No. 30794 Sir
Ector de Maris stands
at the night ferry's
traditional platform 2
at London Victoria.

● **BOTTOM
RIGHT**
The up Continental
boat express leaving
Dover Marine station
after collecting
passengers from the
cross-channel ferry.

Depression had persuaded the railway
company that their only course of action
was to admit second-class passengers.

Sporting a Union Flag and Tricolour,
the Golden Arrow departed London
Victoria at 11.00 a.m. The journey began
with a 1:62 climb on to the Grosvenor
Bridge. Subsequent gradients included
2.4 km (1½ miles) at 1:102 leading to
Penge tunnel, and 3 km (2 miles) at 1:95
to Bickley Junction, with slow running
round the curve to Orpington.

Just before reaching Tonbridge the
train was faced with 6 km (4 miles) at
1:122 and 3 km (2 miles) at 1:144, the
latter through the Sevenoaks tunnel.
From here to Dover Marine, reached at
12.38, the line was level and speeds of 96
kph (60 mph) were possible.

The ferry, Canterbury, crossed the
English Channel in 75 minutes. After
transferring to the awaiting Flèche d'Or,
a four-cylinder Nord Pacific of the
French Northern Railway, the travellers
completed the last 296 km (184 miles)
from Calais to Paris in 190 minutes,
arriving in the French capital at 17.35.
You can still travel by rail and ferry from
Victoria to Paris, but not by steam.

BEDFORD TO BLETCHLEY

A rail journey from Bedford to Bletchley, two stations that connect the Midland main line with the West Coast main line, may not sound as romantic as a trip on the Orient Express, but the "friendly line", as many locals call it, is one of the finest journeys in the kingdom.

Since the first train ran on 17 November 1846, operated by the London & North Western Railway, the line has been vital to the people of the area. A journey along the route engineered by George and Robert Stephenson, now denominated the Marston Vale line and operated by National Express, is like a trip back to the 1930s. The 27 km (17 mile) journey,

which takes 50 minutes, is completely rural, with no mass urbanization to be seen. There are three manned level crossings and no fewer than six signal boxes that still operate semaphore signals. The Fenny Stratford box houses a fine collection of old paintings and sepia photographs showing the area as it was.

At the beginning of the 20th century, the line was covered by a railmotor service. These were an early form of multiple unit and consisted of a self-propelled coach fitted with a steam boiler in one end. Because the passengers entered and left the coaches by means of steps, it was not necessary to build conventional platforms at the halts along the way. Today the trains are operated by Heritage DMUs. This is one of the last lines to use these units, which date back to the 1960s.

The journey begins at Bedford Midland station, which is on the Midland main line with services to Luton and Gatwick airports. The first part of the journey passes through Bedford St Johns, Kempston Hardwick, Stewartby (formerly Wootton Pillinge) and Millbrook. Here there is a crossing where the levers are housed in the open air by the side of the box. The crossing keeper has a collection of wheel hub caps that have fallen off cars as they ride over the bumpy crossing.

Part of the route goes over land belonging to the Duke of Bedford. The 10th Duke was a great supporter of the building of the line. He did, however,

● **ABOVE RIGHT**
Evening shadows lengthen as the two-car Class 117 DMU ambles through glorious countryside near Millbrook with a Bletchley to Bedford service.

● **RIGHT**
A Bletchley-bound train pauses at the delightful rural station of Fenny Compton, next to the A5 Watling Street, with a Bletchley to Bedford service. Note the semaphore signals and the high escarpment sweeping towards Ampthill in the background.

INFORMATION BOX

Termini	Bedford and Bletchley
Country	England
Distance	27 km (17 miles)
Date of opening	1846

insist that all the station buildings on his estate (Fenny Stratford, Woburn Sands, Ridgmont and Millbrook) should be of half-timber design. Woburn Sands, the coal depot for the line, was also important for its brickyard, and the railway was used to transport the bricks.

A feature of the journey used to be the London Brick Works, whose many tall chimneys were counted by generations of children. There are now only ten, which can still be seen from the train. The old clay pits, now filled with water, create a moonlike landscape. Some of these sites were used as landfill for London's waste, which was carried down the line as far as Forders Sidings.

● **ABOVE**
The Derby Lightweight two-car DMU Class 108 stands in the bay at Bedford station with a Class 319 Thameslink EMU in the background.

● **ABOVE RIGHT**
The traditional country station atmosphere of the 1930s is conjured up in this typical scene as a two-car Class 108 unit stands at Aspley Guise station.

● **RIGHT**
"Ten Chimneys". A two-car Class 117 DMU ambles past the high escarpment near Lidlington with a Bedford to Bletchley service.

LONDON TO COLOGNE

There are three rail routes from London to Cologne. One is via the Hook of Holland, one is via Ostend, and the third is through the Channel Tunnel.

● **VIA THE HOOK OF HOLLAND**

This used to be one of the pleasantest ways to go to Cologne. A boat train, usually with the best stock the railway could muster and a gleaming locomotive at the head, left London's Liverpool Street station each evening. On arrival at the special station at Harwich, where facilities have been greatly improved recently, passengers passed through passport and customs controls and walked straight to the ship. This route can still be followed, but since June 1997 night ships for rail passengers have been discontinued and replaced by catamarans operating day services only.

The railway station at the Hook of Holland is on the dockside. Connecting international express trains ceased a few years ago and the route via Venlo now requires a couple of changes to get to Cologne. Frequent local services run to Rotterdam, which is a major port.

● **LEFT**
The König Albert was one of the vessels that ferried passengers from Dover to Ostend in the 1950s.

INFORMATION BOX

Termini	London and Cologne
Countries	England, Belgium, Netherlands and Germany
Distance	via Ostend 595 km (370 miles); via The Hook of Holland 545 km (339 miles)
Date of opening	via Ostend 1861; via The Hook of Holland 1893; via the Channel Tunnel 1994

● **LEFT**
The Hook of Holland rail/ship station by night. The large ships will soon be replaced by large catamarans.

● LEFT
Ostend station.

The terrain in the Netherlands is only difficult for rail construction to the extent that numerous rivers, many of them navigable, must be crossed. On the line to Venlo is the longest rail bridge in the Netherlands, at 1.07 km (3,510 ft), over the Hollandsch Diep at Moerdijk. Other places of rail interest are Tilburg, where the main workshops of the Netherlands railways are situated, and Venlo, on the border with Germany, an industrial centre that not only provides a wide variety of Netherlands motive power but also sees the hand-over of trains to German locomotives.

The route through Utrecht is the one now normally used to get to Cologne from Rotterdam. There is a good connecting train every hour to Utrecht, a major rail junction.

● **VIA OSTEND**

London's Victoria station was the starting-point to this once classic route to the continent, with boat trains depositing passengers virtually alongside ships. Today an electric multiple unit (EMU) runs to Ramsgate, and the bus provided by the shipping line carries passengers to the harbour. The night crossing used to bring them to Ostend early enough to catch the 06.34 train, giving passengers an arrival at Cologne by 10.42. The harbour at Ostend is host to myriad small

● **BELOW**
The smart way to get to Brussels and into Germany is to come from England by Eurostar from Waterloo station in London. A train arrives at Brussels Midi station, where connections can readily be made to most parts of Europe.

craft and fishing boats, and the town can offer a variety of places to sample continental fare. Just outside the station, a coastal tramway, part of the much diminished "Vicinal" system, runs southwards to De Panne and northwards to Knokke.

The elegant building and seven platforms of Ostend station are right alongside the quay. In addition to the usual local and inter-city services, international trains commence their journeys here, although the numbers have declined in recent years. At Ghent, the largest town in 13th-century Europe, there is a large railway station with an

● **LEFT**
A Sprinter on local services stands at Rotterdam Central station.

● RIGHT
Cologne's Hauptbahnhof is overshadowed by
the city's Gothic cathedral.

impressive old main building. In the early
morning and evening rush hours its many
tracks are very busy. A good range of
motive power and a variety of EMUs plus
the occasional freight train provide
constant interest.

And so to Brussels where the third
and possibly best railway route to
Cologne is met.

● VIA THE CHANNEL TUNNEL

Waterloo station in London houses a fine
modern terminal for the Eurostar trains,
which serve Paris, Lille and Brussels.
Passport and other checks take place in
the commodious hall beneath the
platforms, which are reached by
escalators. The interior of the trains bears
a close resemblance to the French TGV
on which it is based. Once under way, the
ride quality is superb. It is so quiet and
smooth that the impression of speed is
hard to determine.

The train makes a slow start from
London, weaving its way through the
suburbs for many kilometres until it can

sprint along the fairly straight route
through Kent, passing hop fields and
oast-houses on the way to the entrance to
Dollands Moor sidings, where the live
current ceases to be collected from a
third rail and is taken from the overhead
line equipment. This operation is carried
out without stopping, and the train is
soon running at the maximum permitted
speed of 160 kph (100 mph) for about
20 minutes through the tunnel.

The train emerges in France with the
very extensive sidings for the car and
goods vehicle shuttle services away to the
left. The TGV line to Lille is joined and
having passed the specially built station
there is a locomotive depot to the right
and a large TGV and general repair depot
to the left. As the high-speed lines in
Belgium are completed it is possible to
see and appreciate the impressive
engineering feats which have been
undertaken in this ambitious project.

Brussels also has a fine Eurostar
terminal at the Midi station. From the
many platforms of the main station,
trains go to all parts of Europe. Below,
trams and a metro system serve the
environs of this bustling capital city.

The Belgium Government was far-
sighted when it supported the joining of
stations north and south of the city by a
tunnel – something yet to be achieved in
Paris or London. Brussel Centraal, as the
name implies, serves the city centre,
where there are many fine buildings. The
Gare du Nord is situated in the French-
speaking part of the city, in an area which
was once rather disreputable but is now
being sanitized by the construction of
many modern buildings.

● **RIGHT**
For passengers with some time to spare there is plenty to see and do in Brussels. Maybe a cup of coffee, or something stronger, in the Grande Place.

● **OPPOSITE BELOW**
The majority of short-distance inter-city and local passenger-trains are in the hands of EMUs in Belgium. Aum 75 Class 4-car unit heads a rush-hour train at Gent St Pieters.

● **BELOW**
The old Marloiban station in Utrecht has been turned into a fine railway museum. Railways in the Netherlands bought many locomotives from the UK. This outside-framed 2-4-0 No. 32 was built by Beyer-Peacock in 1864.

● **BOTTOM**
German Railways No. 140. 741 stands at the Dutch/German border at Venlo. It has taken over from its German counterpart and will soon set off for Cologne.

There are numerous trains from Midi station to Cologne, taking just under three hours, but this timing will be greatly reduced when the planned new lines have been completed. The approach by rail to Liège is down a very steep gradient, and even today a special electric locomotive is kept to bank heavy trains going in the Brussels direction. The station is very busy, with trains coming from all points of the compass, including the picturesque line to Luxembourg. The line climbs away from Liège following a sinuous course with some pleasant scenery on the way to Aachen. Beyond Aachen, the journey is largely through rural agricultural areas, passing the significant town of Düren. Increasing industry and urbanization heralds arrival at the outskirts of Cologne with large carriage sidings to the right and a massive locomotive depot at the left.

Cologne's main station is at a high level on the banks of the River Rhine. Its huge arched roof shelters passenger-trains of all descriptions, and traffic has increased to such an extent that the Hohenzollern bridge across the river now has a modern double track set of spans opposite the spans of the road and tramway part of the bridge that was destroyed in World War II.

PARIS TO ISTANBUL
THE ORIENT EXPRESS

● OPPOSITE

A Kraus-Maffei Bavarian 18 Class 4-6-2,
No. 18470 L63, hauling the Orient Express
between Kehl and Stuttgart in about 1933.

What became the Orient Express sprang
upon eight countries in 1883. Founded
specially by Georges Nagelmackers, a
Belgian mining engineer, La Compagnie
Internationale des Wagons-Lits (The
International Sleeping Car Company),
the world's first multi-national, had been
running through sleeping cars with wide
buffers from Paris to Vienna since 1876.
"Et des Grands Express Européens" was
added to the name in 1883 when the
train first linked Paris with Bucharest, as
it still does today, via Munich, Vienna and
Budapest. The journey took 77 hours
one way and 81 the other – local time
was unsynchronized.

Istanbul passengers were taken on to
Giurgiu, ferried from Romania across the
river Danube to Rustchuk in Bulgaria and
then had another seven-hour train
journey to the Black Sea port of Varna.
From here an Austrian Lloyd liner took
the travellers on the final part of their
82-hour journey.

From 8 August 1888, the train
abandoned Giurgiu and diverted at
Budapest to Belgrade and Nis in Serbia.
It then travelled up the Dragoman Pass
through the Northern Passara mountains
by cornice and tunnel, on a gradient of
1:37, to Bulgaria; down to Sofia, up again

● **ABOVE**
The Military Orient Express in 1919. All the
seats on this Allied military train were held by
the French Army, but civilians were admitted if
seats were available. It is seen here crossing
the River Limmat near Zurich.

● **BELOW**
The Orient Express as seen on the French
Eastern Railway on 4 October 1883. The train
of two passenger cars and a sleeper is being
hauled by a 500 Class 2-4-0.

INFORMATION BOX

THE ORIENT EXPRESS

Termini	Paris and Istanbul
Countries	France to Turkey
Distance	3,212 km (1,996 miles)
Date of opening	1883

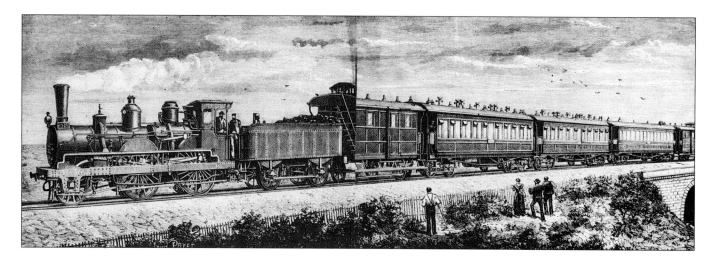

to Tatar Pazardjik, and through the mountains over the newly opened line to the city of Plovdiv, the furthermost point of the Oriental Railway from Istanbul. This journey took 67 hours and a few minutes.

Passengers from 1888 enjoyed the comfortable sleeping cars with velvet curtains, plush seating, lavatories at the car ends, and a tinkling hand-bell in the corridors, which summoned them to five-course French *haute cuisine* in the dining cars. Renamed the Orient Express in 1891, it made cursory frontier stops

to change engines. The clientele always included government couriers, chained to their diplomatic bags, but often royalty and diplomats also used the train. Indeed the story goes that a Romanian count caught the train just to enjoy the menu, remarking, "The express takes four hours to cross me" – meaning his vast estate!

Leaving Gare de l'Est, Paris, the train had an easy run up the Marne valley through Champagne vineyards, Epernay and Chalons, where, later, the Calais car was attached. The train then crossed the River Moselle at Nancy and continued on its way to the then German frontier at Deutsch-Avricourt.

The route across Alsace passes through the notable 1,678 m (5,505 ft)

● **ABOVE RIGHT**
One of the head attendants waits to welcome passengers aboard the Orient Express.

● **ABOVE**
The Pullman coat of arms.

● **RIGHT**
A British Pullman, taken at Kensington Olympia around 1987. The train manager stands in front of the dining car.

● LEFT
The Orient Express in Turkey about 1910. The train here is being hauled by an Oriental Railways Austrian-built 4-4-0. Note the "cow-catcher" on the locomotive.

The Orient Express was stopped abruptly in 1914 by the outbreak of World War I, when both sides used were forced to commission their passenger coaches for use as ambulance trains.

In 1916 the Germans started the rival Mitropa Company, using requisitioned Wagons-Lits cars, running the Berlin-Istanbul Balkan Express, to reach their Turkish allies. After the 1918 Armistice was signed in Wagons-Lits Dining Car No. 2419, destroyed by Hitler's SS troops in 1944, the Orient Express restarted with difficulty in 1921. In 1923, due to the Rheinland Occupation, the train was diverted via Zurich (Switzerland) and the 10.24 km (6 miles 650 yd) long Austrian Arlberg tunnel, which had been completed in 1884. This became a permanent route.

The Swiss-Arlberg-Vienna Express, renamed Arlberg-Orient Express in 1932, ran to Budapest via Hagyeshalom from Vienna, and to Bucharest via Sighisoara. A Paris-Athens sleeper ran

long Homarting-Arzviller twin tunnels – the twin carries the Marne-Rhein Canal. Eight km (5 miles) beyond Strasbourg (Strassburg) the Orient Express crossed the Rhine at Kehl, over a steel bridge destroyed in World War II, into Baden-Württemberg.

After travelling through Stuttgart, Augsburg and Ulm the express arrived in Bavaria's capital, Munich. Originally the express entered Austria at Simbach, but was soon diverted past Lake Prien to Salzburg and so on to Vienna, where, from 1894, it was joined by the Ostend-Vienna express.

The Orient Express then ran on through Bratislava to Budapest. The next section of the route, through to Bucharest, was via Szged and Timisoara, over the now disused 30 m (99 ft) high Biatorbagy viaduct, where, in 1931, the train was dramatically blown up by Czech fascists.

The Istanbul train ran south from Budapest, crossing the Danube at Peiterwarden bridge, and the Serbian frontier at Subotica. From here it was an easy run, through fields of sunflowers, to Nis-Plovdiv and the junction for Greece.

From Plovdiv, the Oriental Railway followed the Maritza valley near the Bulgarian frontier and so, after crossing the river several times, once over the

1,270 m (4,167 ft) long, 173-span bridge at Pithion, the train ran along the dramatic Aegean coastline to Thessalonika. It was on this stretch of the line that Ian Fleming's *From Russia with Love* was filmed. Then there are 1:66 gradients over the snow-clad hills to the Sea of Marmora and journey's end at Istanbul's Sirkeci station.

In 1900 Wagon-Lits tried a Berlin-Breslau (Wroclaw) to Istanbul express that avoided Vienna. This experiment, however, sadly only lasted two years.

● LEFT
An exterior view of
one of the Pullman
coaches, which form
the legendary train.

twice a week and a Paris-Istanbul service
ran three times a week.

Disrupted again by World War II
(there was a Zurich–Istanbul service for a
time), the Orient Express was restarted
in 1947 with ordinary coaches, one or
two sleepers and the occasional dining
car. In 1950, Captain Karpe, US Military
Attaché at Bucharest, was murdered on
the train as it was passing through a
tunnel near Salzburg, in Russian-
occupied Austria.

The Budapest-Belgrade sector ceased
in 1963 when the Tauern-Orient sleeper
was started from Ostend to Athens. This
ended in 1976. The Tauern tunnel,
which is 8.53 km (5 miles and 557 yd)
long, was completed in 1909.

Today Wagons-Lits Austria still staff
the Vienna-Paris sleeper, while a
Hungarian Railways (MAV) dining car
serves classic dinners between Budapest
and Salzburg. Romanian Railways run the
Budapest-Bucharest sleeper.

● ABOVE
Two stewards pose beside the open doors of
the coaches of the Orient Express.

● RIGHT
Passengers dine in luxury aboard the
Orient Express.

● OPPOSITE
The Arlberg-Orient Express at St Anton in the
Austrian Arlberg in about 1932. Hauled by a
ÖBB locomotive, the train has just emerged
from the Arlberg tunnel.

CALAIS TO ISTANBUL
THE SIMPLON-ORIENT EXPRESS

In 1906, Wagons-Lits started the Simplon Express (SE) from Paris to Lausanne (Switzerland). The route took in the recently opened 19.8 km (12 miles 557 yd) long Simplon Tunnel (Europe's longest until 1991), Milan (Italy) and later Venice (Italy) and Trieste (at that time part of Austria). However, Vienna would not let it proceed farther east, which was precisely the SE objective.

At the end of World War I, the Allied governments at the Treaty of Versailles created the Simplon-Orient Express (SOE). They asked Wagons-Lits to run the route, which connected liberated Romania, Yugoslavia and Athens with the West, thereby avoiding Germany, Austria and Hungary. They also compelled the Germans to restart the Orient Express.

● **LEFT**
A replica of car No. 2439. The original, in which the Armistices of 1918 and 1940 were signed, went by road to Germany, where it was destroyed on the orders of Hitler.

● **BELOW**
The Simplon-Orient Express at the Turkish frontier in 1950.

INFORMATION BOX

THE SIMPLON-ORIENT EXPRESS

Termini	Calais and Istanbul
Countries	France to Turkey
Distance	about 3,460 km (2,150 miles)
Date of opening	1906

The Athens-Salonika main line, with its numerous tunnels and viaducts through and over the Greek mountains, opened in 1917. The second track tunnel was opened in 1921.

The line from Calais Maritime to Paris Gare de Lyon opened in 1870 and crossed the 30 m (99 ft) high Chantilly viaduct. From Paris the Simplon Express followed the Seine valley to the Laroche-Migennes engine-changing stop, after which there was an easy rising gradient to

● **OPPOSITE**
The Venice Simplon-Orient Express travelling through the Arlberg Pass near the picturesque village of Pettnau.

● **LEFT**
The Venice Simplon-Orient Express at Pettnau on the Arlberg in July 1984. The train is headed by ÖBB 1020 and 1010 Class locomotives.

After crossing the Orbe on the 30 m (100 ft) high Le Day bridge, at Daillens, the train joined the Swiss main line, electrified in 1906, from Neuchâtel to Lausanne, continuing along Lake Geneva through Montreux and following the Rhône valley to Brig at the mouth of the Simplon Tunnel. This last section was electrified in 1906.

The line emerged at Iselle, Italy, from where the Swiss-operated line drops 358 m (1,175 ft) in 28 km (17 miles) through the Trasquera tunnel, Iselle station, the 2,968 m (9,738 ft) long Varzo Spiral tunnel, five smaller tunnels and the 1,092 m (3,583 ft) long Preglia tunnel, to join the Italian railways at Domodossola. Passing Lake Maggiore, the train followed the flat line, built in

the Blaizy-Bas summit and a 4,100 m (13,451 ft) long tunnel before descending to Dijon. Here, turning east from Burgundy, it climbed from 288 m (945 ft) at Mouchard to 900 m (2,953 ft) at the mouth of the 6,100 m (20,013 ft) long Mont d'Or Tunnel, opened in

1915, which goes through the Jura mountains to Vallorbe (Switzerland). Before the tunnel was built, the trains ran via Pontarlier to Vallorbe on a line, which is now disused but whose claim to fame is that, in 1974, the film *Murder on the Orient Express* was made on it.

1848, from Milan to Venice, passing Lake Garda and Verona. After reversing at Venice the train crossed the causeway to Venice-Mestre, where the line rejoined the coast outside Trieste.

The Simplon-Orient Express, with its teak cars, took three nights and four days each way. Although all passengers had to change at Trieste, westbound passengers could sleep in the standing train and catch the connection to Paris the following morning.

From Trieste, where all passengers had to change, the line climbed from sea-level to 302 m (991 ft) at Poggioreale del Carso, the present frontier.

The SOE route through Ljubljana (Laibach) and Zagreb (Agram) ran daily to Vinkovci-Belgrade and Nis, where it divided — one part going to Istanbul (three times weekly) and the other to Athens (twice weekly). The Istanbul train also had connections to Bucharest, which it reached by using the notorious Vinkovci-Subotica branch line that crossed the Yugoslav-Romanian frontier over the Danube near the Iron Gates. Fuel shortages sometimes caused delays,

indeed it is said that on one occasion the passengers had to put money together to buy wood for the engine!

The famous blue-and-gold all-steel sleepers first appeared in 1926, four years after the Train Bleu (Calais-Nice-San Remo). By 1929 there was a daily service from Paris to Istanbul, which included a dining car, Calais-Istanbul sleepers and Calais-Trieste sleepers. In 1930 the SOE became the main prop of the Wagons-Lits London-Cairo service (known as the Taurus Express).

The train was re-organized in 1932, with the Ostend-, Amsterdam-, Berlin-, Prague-, Vienna-, and Paris-Orient or Arlberg-Orient sleepers joining the train at Belgrade on different days. This provided three daily Istanbul sleepers and two services daily (four from Thessaloniki) to Athens.

Romantic, dazzlingly mysterious, the train was used by all the Balkan grandees. King Boris used to drive the Simplon-Orient's engine in Bulgaria. British agents

● **ABOVE**
This rare picture shows the Venice Simplon-Orient Express on a diversion on the old Arlberg-Orient Express line via Zell am See. This was caused by a damaged bridge at Kufstein. The train is seen here in the 180 degree turn near Hopfgarten in Tyrol in July 1990.

● **RIGHT**
The Venice Simplon-Orient Express stands at Jenbach station in the Austrian Tyrol. A storm is brewing over the mountains.

● **RIGHT**
The Venice Simplon-Orient Express at St Jodock, between Brenner and Innsbruck.

● **BELOW LEFT**
This pre-war scene shows the Simplon-Orient Express on the Gorgopotamos bridge in Greece.

included Lord Baden-Powell, later founder of the Boy Scouts movement. It was on the train, just after World War II broke out, that Royal Navy agents murdered a German agent. Many novels were written about the train, perhaps most famously Agatha Christie's *Murder on the Orient Express* and Graham Greene's *Stamboul Train*. Mystery also reflected the route's atmosphere, in which there were always difficulties with the local customs, who sealed one dining car's cupboard supplies and broke the seals on another at each border.

Wagons-Lits kept reserve supplies of block ice, coal and vehicles along the route, maintaining an almost out-of-this-world glamorous elegance on board. In summer the baggage van had a shower in it. Wagons-Lits ran daily dining cars for Lausanne-Trieste-Svilengrad, Nis-Thessaloniki, Amfiklia-Athens and a kitchen van for Uzunkopru-Istanbul.

World War II did not stop the Simplon-Orient's glamorous journeys. The warning that "Les Oreilles de l'ennemi vous écoutent" (the equivalent of the British World War II poster

"Walls have Ears") was pasted in the cabins – the listening enemy ears still travelling in the Berlin car, which lasted until 1940. The train was finally stopped in 1942, and individual sleepers with neutral Turkish staff served most of the overnight sectors until the SOE re-started in January 1946 (to Istanbul) and 1949 (Athens). After the war, dining cars became a rarity.

The Simplon-Orient Express ended in 1962, and, with much media coverage, the last Paris-Istanbul sleeper ran on 22 May 1977.

● **RIGHT**
This 1907 photograph shows the Venice Simplon-Orient Express, headed by a Swiss steam-engine, at Iselle di Trasquera at the Italian portal of the Simplon tunnel.

GORNERGRAT TO ST MORITZ
THE GLACIER EXPRESS

Most people start this journey at Zermatt or St Moritz, but to miss seeing the Matterhorn while standing amid the snow 3,000 m (10,000 ft) up, with a panoramic view of other mountains, is to miss one of the finer sights in Europe.

It is not essential to take the Glacier Express itself to enjoy the wonderful scenery, but there are a number of advantages such as the provision of air-conditioned Panorama coaches and a restaurant car in which one can experience the novelty of having a wine glass with an angled base so that the stem and bowl remain upright on the steep gradients. It is recommended that, if at all possible, a seat is obtained on the right-hand side facing forward on this part of the journey.

There is pasture land in the valley from here to Randa. Look out for the houses built behind the huge boulders that fell from the mountains many years before. The Weisshorn, 4,506 m (14,783 ft) is off to the left. Between Randa and Herbriggen is a new section of rack line

A heavy express from Chur to St Moritz with coaches from the "Glacier Express" is about to plunge into the tunnel in the vertical rockface 213 feet above the Landwasser river.

● **BELOW LEFT**
A train from Chur to Arosa eases round the bend in the road by the Obertor gate in the city walls of Chur to join road traffic on the narrow Plessurquai alongside the river.

● **BELOW RIGHT**
The Gornergratbahn rack railway train is completing its descent to Zermatt. An electric taxi makes its almost silent way to a hotel.

Swiss Federal Railways main line down the Rhône valley. A short, brisk run on level ground brings the train to Brig. Watch out on the left for the trains of the Bern-Loetschberg-Simplon railway clinging to the valley side on their way to and from the Lötschberg tunnel.

Like most other towns strategically situated near the entrance to mountain passes, Brig has a long history and today watches over the northern entrance to the Simplon railway tunnel beneath the pass of the the same name, which links Switzerland with Italy. It has strong commercial and industrial interests and a growing tourist trade.

At Brig the train reverses in the station square outside the impressive Federal Railways building. A locomotive of the

constructed in the past ten years to circumvent the area where the whole mountainside collapsed, fortunately without causing any loss of life. This can be seen to the left where the route of the old line can still be seen in places.

The valley descends in steps at one place near Kalpetran, the line sharing a narrow gorge with the river. It then appears that the broadening valley with pastures and small vineyards heralds the end of spectacular views for the moment. Not so, for suddenly the train is perched on the edge of a deep cleft cut by the river, and following the contours, wheel flanges screaming.

Ahead and to the right appear two bridges leaping across the chasm. Both were built to carry the road from

Stalden-Saas, which the train is now approaching, to Saas-Fee.

The valley becomes wider and more populous, and at the large town of Visp the line shares a station area with the

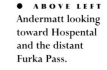

● ABOVE LEFT
Andermatt looking toward Hospental and the distant Furka Pass.

● LEFT
The young Vorderrhein rushes alongside the line as both descend toward Hospental. In the far distance, road and rail zigzag up the mountainside from Andermatt heading for Disentis.

INFORMATION BOX

THE GLACIER EXPRESS

Termini	Gornergrat and St Moritz
Country	Switzerland
Distance	279 km (173 miles)
Date of opening	1926

The imposing Swiss Federal Railways station at Brig forms a fine backdrop to the station shared by the Furka-Oberalp and Brig-Visp-Zermatt railways. The "Glacier Express" reverses here.

using rack-and-pinion gear to climb. Be ready to look out to the right on emerging from the tunnel, for there is a wonderful view back down the valley toward Brig.

Lax sees the end of the rack for the present. Fiesch is a pretty tourist town in a sheltered location, from here the railway executes a 180 degree climbing turn on rack away from the town to reach Frgangen and yet another cable-car to Bellwald and the Fiesch glacier. One of the most picturesque parts of the journey follows as the train passes through or near many charming old villages, with their wooden houses packed closely together for shelter from the elements, watched over by an ancient church. Look out for the ancient wooden barns, which are raised above the ground on supports capped by large flat stones to prevent rats and mice from reaching the stored grain and fodder above.

At Oberwald, the present-day railway parts company from the old line. The latter passed Gletsch, with splendid views of the Rhône Glacier, the source of the

● RIGHT
Horse-drawn transport vies for business with battery-electric taxis outside the Zermatt station of the Brig-Visp-Zermatt railway. The station has been rebuilt since the picture was taken.

● BELOW RIGHT
The clear waters of the Matter Vispa tumble alongside a Zermatt to Brig train as it approaches Täsch station.

Furka-Oberalp (FO) Railway takes over, probably one of the 64 tonne (63 ton) rack-and-adhesion machines introduced in 1986.

Immediately after passing the BVZ locomotive depot at the station, the train swings right to cross the Rhône, known locally as the Rotten, on a girder bridge. Another sharp right turn, and the train is running alongside one of the main streets in Naters, just across from Brig. The valley narrows and is shared by road, rail and river.

Grengiols has the highest viaduct on the FO, it spans 31 m (102 ft) above the valley floor. When the train has crossed the viaduct, it enters a spiral tunnel still

● LEFT
The autumn tints are still on the trees as one of
the new and powerful locomotives of the
Rhaetischebahnen climbs with its train away
from Tiefencastel on its way to St Moritz.

and, of course, there are the regular
passenger-trains. About two-thirds of the
way through the tunnel, the train is
under the watershed of the Rhône and
Reuss rivers.

The line emerges near Realp and
follows the broad Urseren valley, passing
Hospental close by on the right.

Andermatt is a well-known holiday
centre and the junction for what used to
be the Schöllenen Bahn, now part of the
FO system. This runs down a steep rack
line in the narrow gorge to Göschenen

river, and entered the old tunnel to
emerge in a wild valley where the winter
conditions are so severe that through rail
services to Andermatt and beyond can be
suspended. Happily, a preservation
society is in the process of re-opening the
line between Gletsch and Realp for
summer use.

The present line uses a new tunnel,
much lower down the mountains. It was
opened on 26 June 1982 after a ten-year
construction period and with a length of
15.442 km (9.59 miles). Single-track
with two passing loops, it is the longest
metre-gauge tunnel in the world. Special
trains ferry cars and their passengers
through the tunnel in winter and summer

● ABOVE
Thusis is an important
rail and road
interchange point on
the line between Chur
and St Moritz. Its new
station reflects the
innovative style of the
Rhaetischebahnen.

● LEFT
Arosa is reached in
less than an hour by
a spectacular branch
of the Rhaetischebahn
from the station
square at Chur.

on the Federal Railways main line
through the Gotthard pass and tunnel.
Glacier expresses cross at Andermatt,
and much shunting is necessary to
change the restaurant car from one train
to the other.

The climb out of Andermatt is both
surprising and rewarding. A seemingly
impassable mountainside faces the train,
which heads straight for it, engages the
rack and swings right, climbing across the
face of the wall and giving views of the
valley to the right. Then it reverses

direction, opening up even wider views down the Urseren valley, now to the left. There are no fewer than four such reversals before reaching Nätschen, which is 407 m (1,335 ft) higher than Andermatt. Still climbing, the train passes through a long avalanche shelter to emerge with the Oberalp lake to the right and, just ahead, the station of Oberalppasshöhe at 2,033 m (6,670 ft) the highest point on the FO.

Between Tschamut and Dieni is the small and isolated chapel of St Brida, built in 1736. From here on there is no need for rack assistance as the valley broadens out with pleasant views. Sedrun is one of the access points for the construction of a new tunnel beneath the Gotthard pass which will revolutionize times on perhaps Europe's most important north-south axis.

Disentis's station has the attraction of being the meeting-point between the FO and Rhaetische Bahn (RhB) where, again, a locomotive change takes place with haulage probably being put into the hands of one of the fairly new 60 tonne (59 ton) Ge4/4 machines. The going is

now easy through pasture dotted with woodland. The next important feature is the Rhine gorge, which is entered around Castrisch, some 2 km (1¼ mile) beyond Ilanz. It was formed in prehistoric times

by a landslide which filled the valley to a depth of 300 m (984 ft) through which the river gradually forced its way. The unusual rock formations are best seen from the left-hand side of the train.

The majority of passengers on the through trains are heading for St Moritz, and the coaches for that destination are detached from the train at Reichenau-Tamins and added to another train that has started at Chur.

Chur, the capital of the canton, is also the terminus of the standard-gauge Federal Railways and has a depot and workshops. The large station, recently rebuilt to incorporate the bus station, is shared by the RhB.

On the way back to Reichenau, the Ems Chemie works at Domat-Ems is seen to the left. For passengers coming direct from Zermatt, there is a further reversal at Reichenau, and after crossing

The line between Disentis and Chur passes along a deep valley cut by the Vorderrhein through the prehistoric Flims landslip.

the Hinterrhein the train swings left to follow its course all the way to Thusis.

As the train climbs away from Thusis, on the right one can glimpse the fearsome Viamala gorge cut by the Hinterrhein, while on the left there is a good view back down the valley. The Schyn gorge cut by the Albula River is now followed right to Preda.

The line holds to the left side of the valley. Suddenly, round a curve, the remarkable Landwasser viaduct appears, carrying the tracks 65 m (213 ft) above the valley floor before plunging into a tunnel cut into the rock face.

Filisur is the junction for the shuttle trains to Davos and the starting-point for one of the most gruelling climbs in Europe for trains relying on adhesion only. It involves brilliant engineering, with the line now clinging to a vertical mountainside, then spiralling across the narrowing valley to gain height and then into spiral tunnels, one upon the other. Between Bergen and Preda at the Albula tunnel, the line rises from 1,376 m (4,514 ft) above sea level to 1,792 m

● LEFT
In February, the snow is beginning to melt on the rooftops of the ancient city of Chur, the capital of the Kanton of Graubünden.

● BELOW LEFT
The upper valley of the Vorderrhein near Tschamut-Selva in the grip of winter.

(5,879 ft) in about 12 km (7.5 miles) with a ruling gradient of 1:28.6. The Albula tunnel is the highest in Europe, with the summit in the tunnel at 1,820 m (5,971 ft). It was built between 1898 and 1902 under impossible conditions and has a length of 5,864.5 m (3^{1}/$_{2}$ miles).

Samedan is a rail junction for Pontresina and the Bernina line and has a locomotive depot and workshops. It is only a short distance to St Moritz, passing through Celerina. The railway ends at St Moritz by the lake used for langlauf in winter. Above the lake are the hotels and restaurants of one of the most famous resorts in the world, a fine centre for exploring Switzerland's mountain scenery.

PILATUS
A ROUND TRIP FROM LUCERNE

● BELOW
The banner at Alpnachstad proclaims that
the Pilatusbahn is the steepest rack railway in
the world. Even the platform at the station is
on a steep gradient.

Few visitors to Lucerne in central
Switzerland can have failed to notice the
imposing bulk of Pilatus, a massif of
limestone virtually in the suburbs of the
city. The massif comprises a number of
peaks, the highest of which is
Tomlishorn, 2,129 m (6,985 ft) high.

The mountain had an attraction for
tourists long before the coming of the
famous Pilatus railway, and several
famous people have made the ascent,
including Queen Victoria in 1868. Even
then, she could obtain refreshment after
the ascent, because two hotels had been
built near the summit in 1860.

The success of the standard-gauge
rack-and-pinion railway from Vitznau to
the summit of the Rigi mountain
prompted an application to the Federal
Parliament in 1873 by the Vitznau-Rigi
board to build a rack-and-pinion line up
Pilatus. This implied using gradients no
steeper than 1:4, the limit imposed by
the Swiss authorities on the grounds that
the vehicles might lift off the rack were
the inclination to be greater. The line
would have followed the route already

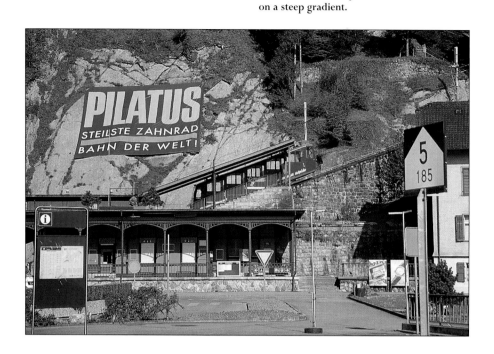

INFORMATION BOX

Terminus	Lucerne
Country	Switzerland
Length	4.27 km (2.65 miles)
Date of opening	1889

● BELOW LEFT
A small plume of cloud adorns the summit of
Pilatus, seen from a ship on Lake Lucerne,
which is heading for Alpnachstad at the foot
of the mountain several kilometres away.

● BELOW RIGHT
Even the steep steps of the station platform
at Alpnachstad fail to convey an adequate
impression of the severity of the gradient
on which the car stands.

● **LEFT**
An ascending car nears the upper station just below the summit of Pilatus.

● **BELOW**
A metre gauge train on the Brünig line of the Federal railways is arriving at Alpnachstad from Lucerne.

● **BELOW**
The car to the left has just departed from Alpnachstad station. Those to the right are waiting to pick up passengers.

used by porters and horses. It was soon realized that this was so circuitous that the heavy construction costs would make it unlikely to return a profit. A shorter route would also be much steeper, and an obvious one was from Alpnachstad by the shores of Lake Lucerne, calling for a gradient of almost 1:2. The Locher rack-and-pinion system based on a concept by the famous mountain railway engineer, Riggenbach, utilizes a pair of vertically mounted pinions which engage in teeth on either side of the rack rail, thus providing a drive and preventing lateral movement. Beneath the teeth on the pinions, discs larger in diameter than the toothed wheels rotate beneath the broad base of the rack rail, thus preventing vertical movement. The conventional wheels on locomotives and carriages merely provide stability on the 800 mm gauge track. Turnouts are always complex on lines such as this, but the Pilatus is special. At six locations, heavy-duty

traverses slide curved track into the appropriate positions, while at two other points, one near the summit, the whole turnout is rotated horizontally.

The line, 4.27 km (2½ miles) long, opened on 4 June 1889 and runs from

Alpnachstad at 441 m (1,447 ft) above sea level to the upper station at 2,070 m (6,791 ft). Between 1886 and 1909, 11 combined steam locomotives and carriages operated the services until electrification at 1550V d.c. on 15 May 1937. One of the steam units is preserved at the transport museum in Lucerne.

Eight electric units were introduced at the start of electrical operation, followed in 1954 by a freight unit, which was provided with a "swap body" to convert it for passenger work, as required, in 1962. One more passenger unit arrived in 1968, and in 1981 another freight unit, diesel-powered, was delivered.

It is suggested that the journey is started at the ship terminus just in front of the main railway terminus at Lucerne and that a ship, possibly one of the old paddle steamers, is taken to Alpnachstad. In summer, there are six or seven sailings a day, and one can enjoy a meal and a drink while admiring the scenery and observing the considerable activity on Lake Lucerne. The alternative is to take the Swiss Federal Railways (SBB) Brünig line metre-gauge train to Alpnachstad.

Both train and ship deposit the passenger close to the Pilatusbahn station. The bright red trains await at a platform angled to correspond with that

of the train. It is advisable to choose the lowest compartment and, if possible, to obtain a seat on the far side facing downhill. Although sitting alongside the rock face on much of the lower part of the journey, you will be on the spectacular side on the upper section, where the line is perched on ledges as it nears the summit. Moreover, it is possible to look back down the line for the whole journey. Although facing rearward is advised, the journey is described as if facing forward. Shortly after the train departs, the depot and workshop are seen to the left. The depot is the only place where the tracks are on the level. Rail access is gained by one of the traverser type turnouts. Very soon the houses, the ship and the Brünig railway line look like small-scale models. Then the line enters beech woods, crosses a small mountain road and begins to dive in and out of a series of short tunnels.

After about eight minutes, the train crosses the Wolfort viaduct, which spans a deep gorge, providing a sudden view to the right and below across the arm of Lake Lucerne on which Alpnachstad is situated and toward the Glärner Alps. The train passes through more short tunnels, after which the nearby scene broadens into pasture dotted with contented cows and alpine flowers. Here at Aemsigen Alp is the passing loop and an opportunity to watch the traverser turnouts in action.

Craggy outcroppings of rock start to appear. The line follows the route of an ancient watercourse and levels out a little before reaching the Mattalp pasture, decked with flowers in summer and often with its own contingent of cows, bells

● **ABOVE LEFT**
The car seen at the cab window is descending and has been passed at the only loop there is on the line.

● **ABOVE RIGHT**
The car has just left the shelter of the summit station at Pilatus.

● **RIGHT**
One of the spectacular views from the top of Pilatus. The cables carry the car on the aerial ropeway, which descends toward Kriens near Lucerne.

● **RIGHT**
The paddle steamer Unterwalden heading
for Alpnachstad is glimpsed from
a descending car.

jangling as they munch contentedly on
the grass. There are few trees here,
merely some stunted pines.

Through a tunnel and what a
sensation! The train is crawling up a
ledge on the sheer rock face of the
Eselwand. Far below, little moving dots
proclaim the presence of walkers on the
mountain tracks, while above lies the col
on which is situated the summit station.
If there is a following train, it may be
possible to watch the changing of the
route by the rotating turnout before your
train enters the covered station.

The saddle of the mountain has been
levelled, and the hotels there provide
restaurants and cafeterias as well as
accommodation. There are numerous
safe and well-made paths giving easy
access to viewpoints, which, in fine
weather, are difficult to beat. One can also
watch arriving and departing trains edging
along the Eselwand in the distance.

An interesting way to return to
Lucerne is to take the large cable-car at
the summit, which, immediately on
departure, crosses an abyss on the east

face of the mountain before dropping
down to Fräkmüntegg. The descent is
quite steep, the car losing 650 m
(2,133 ft) in a distance of 1,450 m
(4,760 ft). There, transfer is made to a
Gondelbahn, the little cars of which

swing just above the tree-tops to Kriens
on the outskirts of Lucerne. Arrival is
close to a trolley-bus route, which runs
to the centre of Lucerne, passing on the
way part of the route of the Kriens-
Luzern-Bahn, an industrial railway.

● **RIGHT**
The hotel and
restaurant near the
summit of Pilatus.

● **LEFT**
The last few yards to
the summit of
Pilatus have to be
tackled on foot.

LONDON WATERLOO TO BERNE
EUROSTAR AND *TGV*

This journey is one of the most technically exciting train routes of modern times. It begins at London's Waterloo station, the award-winning, specially built terminal for the Eurostar trains, which currently run regularly via the Channel Tunnel to terminals at Brussels and Paris.

Access to the passenger assembly hall for the Eurostar trains is gained through barriers where special tickets are scanned automatically. If they are valid, they cause gates to open directly to the security examination. First-class passengers are greeted by their steward at the entry to each coach, and there is help available, if needed, for all other passengers.

The international group responsible for design adopted the principles employed in the French TGV (Train Grande Vitesse), but numerous changes were necessary. The trains needed to operate in the much more restricted loading gauge found in Britain; electrical supply was to come from three different systems, including current collection from a third rail in Britain; there were to be four signalling systems; and stringent safety standards were demanded for operation through the tunnel.

The exterior design was British, one consequence of which is that future TGV and the "Thalys" have a central driving

● **ABOVE AND LEFT**
The impressive, lofty Eurostar terminal at Waterloo station, London.

INFORMATION BOX

Termini	London Waterloo and Berne
Countries	England to Switzerland
Distance	1008 km (626 miles)
Date of opening	Eurostar (London to Paris) 1994; TGV (Paris to Berne) 1987

position and one window at the front of
the cab. The interior design was a joint
Franco-Belgian operation, and the result
appears to be that the Eurostar has more
space than the TGV, in spite of being
dimensionally smaller.

There were many mechanical and
electrical problems to be solved. For
example, safety requirements for the
tunnel demanded that passengers could
be moved from one end of the whole
train to the other. That ruled out
employing two units, so that the Eurostar
has just two power cars, situated at each
end of the 20-vehicle formation, with
additional motored bogies under the first
and last passenger coach to make up to
some extent for the loss of the power
that two equivalent TGV sets would
have had.

Bogies had to be reduced in overall
dimensions; the high overhead contact
line in the tunnel called for a higher-
reaching pantograph; carriage steps had
to be designed to match automatically the
differing heights of platforms in three
countries, and the complex signalling
requirements had to be met.

It is a credit to the international teams
that this was all achieved between
conception in 1987 and the start of
regular services in November 1994.

As yet, there is no dedicated high-
speed line in Britain, so the Eurostar
trains have to slot into the slower traffic
found in the south-east of the country. In
the urban area of London, lines built in
the earliest days of railways tend to be

sinuous, but at least it gives the traveller
the opportunity to glimpse the widely
changing patterns of life to be found in
any major city. Once into the Kentish
countryside, there is the opportunity to
increase the speed to 160 kph (100 mph),
especially on the fairly straight section
from Tonbridge to Ashford.

Certain Eurostar trains stop at the
rebuilt station in Ashford, which also

serves local and inter-city trains. This facilitates rail interchange and the gathering of passengers who have come by car and who would not have found it convenient to board in London.

It is a fairly short distance to the point at which the train swings left from the former British Rail lines to those of Eurotunnel. The expanse of tracks, sidings, depots and loading docks for cars and heavy goods vehicles is called Dollands Moor. It is here that the shoes collecting current from the third rail are lifted and the pantograph is raised, although passengers will be unaware of it. The Channel Tunnel is 49.93 km (31.03 miles) long and is the second longest rail tunnel in the world, as well as the tunnel with the longest underwater section. It lies 137.4 m (451 ft) below mean sea level.

French cab signalling passes instructions to trains in the tunnel and on the TGV lines beyond. Maximum speed in the tunnel is restricted to 160 kph (100 mph), and the riding is so smooth that, without any exterior point of reference, it is hard to detect movement.

Passage through the Channel Tunnel takes some 20 minutes and, on emerging from the tunnel into France, the immense yards of the Coquelles terminal can be seen to the left. The line to Paris passes through a newly built exchange station at Fréthun, and soon the Eurostar is running on the high-speed tracks through fairly level terrain with sweeping curves. On this stretch, an announcement is usually made that the train is running at its maximum authorized speed of 300 kph (186.4 mph).

Facilities for departing Eurostar passengers at the Gare du Nord generally leave much to be desired. Those passing

through Paris on their way to Switzerland can either take a taxi (and make sure that it is an official one) to the large and impressive Gare de Lyon or take the relatively new underground link, which gets one there quicker and much more cheaply in some 15 minutes.

Finding the Swiss TGV – and it will probably be Swiss-owned, albeit in standard TGV livery – can be daunting among all the other TGVs, but once on board you can spot the differences between Eurostars and TGVs, which, for example, are wider and higher. The start from the Gare de Lyon is relatively cautious as the TGVs share the tracks with numerous EMU, locomotive-powered push-and-pull services, both often formed of double-deck coaches, and the occasional locomotive-hauled express. As speed picks up, the train passes the immense marshalling yards at Villeneuve St Georges.

At Lieusaint the TGV joins the "Ligne à Grande Vitesse" (LGV), for the most part a new formation and alignment, purpose-built to permit the high-speed performance of these trains to be exploited. This is the Sud-Est LGV to Lyons, Valence and, ultimately, Marseilles.

The services to Berne and Lausanne follow the line only as far as Passilly, from where there is a short link to the old main line at Aisy. Travel on the LGV is so smooth that the train's speed is hard to judge. There is little chance to study the local scene, however, because of the speed and the fact that the line is often in a cutting.

From Aisy to Dijon the alignment is good enough to maintain a good pace, and soon, a little to the right and below, Dijon comes into view. The TGV swings down the long grade, a stern test for man and machine northbound in the days of steam, and enters the busy main station, which is on a rather constricted site. The best trains take only 99 minutes to travel

● **LEFT**
A TGV in orange livery passes the exit of the huge marshalling yards at Villeneuve St Georges in the suburbs of Paris. Several TGV services now bypass this section of line using a new and much quicker route designed for TGVs, partly in tunnel, to reach southbound TGV lines.

● **RIGHT**
View of the Münster
in Berne from the
Kirchenfeld bridge
over the Aare.

● **BELOW
RIGHT**
Some light railways
in Berne terminate
in the streets. This
train has arrived
from Worb, a large
village outside
Berne, and is
waiting in Helvetia
Platz to return to
Worb. The service
has recently been
extended to a
terminal the other
side of the River
Aare at Casino Platz.

plain until it approaches the formidable mountain barrier of the Montagne du Lermont. The narrow defile through the mountains is guarded by the ancient town of Pontarlier, with its impressive castles perched high above rail and road as the Franco-Swiss border is approached.

The first village on Swiss soil is Les Verrières. A little further on and to the right, St Sulpice and Fleurier can be seen below in the Val de Travers, where the Scots engineer, MacAdam, saw the potential of the tar substance mined there as a surface for roads. The line winds through delightful scenery until, suddenly, panoramic views across Lake Neuchâtel are revealed to the right, the lake surface below dotted with yachts, small craft and passenger boats on regular services.

Neuchâtel, whose castle can be seen to the right on the approach, is an ancient city lying on the important main line between Basle and Lausanne/Geneva. Its large station mainly handles trains belonging to the Federal Railways

the 315 km (195.7 miles) from Paris to Dijon.

Soon after leaving Dijon, the TGV swings left away from the broad valley of the Saône and climbs toward the mountains, giving extensive views to the right. These give way to more restricted views as the track gets higher and woods and rocky cuttings close in.

Frasne, on a high plateau, is a junction. The main line runs straight ahead to Vallorbe, just over the Swiss border, from where it swings down with good views across villages and agricultural land until reaching Lake Geneva (Lac Léman) at Lausanne. The other line branches left and meanders across the

(SBB/CFF/FFS), but the livery of the
Berne-Loetschberg-Simplon Railway
(BLS) is also present. It is that company's
metals that are used to cross the generally
level and fertile broad plateau to Berne,
where the TGV service terminates in the
curving and rather gloomy station, well
situated near the centre of this small and
very pleasant capital city.

The journey from Paris has taken 4
hours and 32 minutes. One can leave
London at the civilized hour of 09.53,
arrive in Paris at 14.08 (Central
European Time), leave at 15.50 and
arrive in Berne at 20.22.

● **ABOVE**
One of the electric
multiple units
arriving at Frasne
station.

● **RIGHT**
In the foreground is
one of the many
decorated fountains
to be found in the
heart of the old city
of Berne.

BUDAPEST TO LAKE BALATON

Budapest boasts three main-line termini, two of grand proportions and often featuring in period films, and Déli Pályaudvar (spelt Pú in timetables), a modern structure without much cover over the platforms. The station is close to Castle Hill and the large tram interchange at Moszkva tér and is thus convenient, although other services start at B. Kelenföld, a large suburban station. First-class travel is advisable and reasonably early arrival at the station is recommended, not only to get the right tickets but also to get a seat.

The train is likely to be hauled by one of the ubiquitous class V43 electric locomotives in a pleasing light-blue livery. The first batch of seven were built by Krupp in Germany, but the rest are from the well-known Hungarian firm of Ganz-Mavag. They are dual voltage but here operate on a supply of 25kV/50Hz providing an hourly rating of 2130 kW.

Loads are relatively light, and speeds, by Western European standards, are

● **ABOVE**
Buda seen from the Fisherman's Bastion on Castle Hill.

moderate, but this has the advantage for the interested traveller that the passing scene may be studied, whether it be architectural, agricultural or human.

The train sets off through the industrial and dormitory suburbs of Buda, keeping to the west of the Danube. It threads its way through the complex of lines serving people and industry before entering flattish countryside with small towns and villages, some of the latter surrounded by small fields worked

INFORMATION BOX

Termini	Budapest and Lake Balaton
Country	Hungary
Distance	399 km (248 miles)
Date of opening	1861

● **ABOVE LEFT**
A Russian-built CoCo diesel electric locomotive stands at Balaton central station, waiting for its next duty on a service to Keszthely.

● **LEFT**
The terminal station at Déli Pályaudvar is the starting-point for the journey to Lake Balaton. One of the ubiquitous Class 43 BB electric locomotives, mostly built in Hungary between 1963 and 1982, is the usual motive power for the main-line trains.

● **RIGHT**
The cool courtyard of this café in old Buda provides a welcome relief from the dry heat of mid-summer.

"privately". In open areas one may see a collective farm enlivened by a few trees but surrounded by flat, tilled soil, but this style of farming is mostly found on the Great Plain to the east.

Streams meander near the line, with areas of marsh as well as tall grasses and some woodland. The 47 km (29 miles) from Budapest brings the traveller to Lake Velence, some 10 km (6 miles) long and shallow. It is seen to the right of the train, and its proximity to the city has attracted the usual lakeside cafés and stalls as well as holiday homes. The north end is a wildlife sanctuary, access to which requires a special permit.

Soon after, one reaches the large town and junction of Székesfehérvár, where connections from the north of the country are made. Only 10 km (6 miles)

further on, and 77 km (48 miles) from Budapest, is Szabadbattyán, the junction where the lines to the north and south of Lake Balaton divide. This train is going south of the lake, and it is around here that the distant hills of Bakony Vértes can first be seen at the right.

It is not until after Balatonalig, 102 km (63 miles) from Budapest, that the blue waters of the lake, dotted with sailing craft, come into view on the right. It is the largest freshwater lake in west and central Europe, 77 km (48 miles) long and very shallow. It is no more than 1.5 m (5 ft) deep on the south side as far out as 1 km (.625 mile) from the shore, and it is said to be only about 3 m (10 ft) deep in the middle.

The north shore of Lake Balaton is significantly different from the south. After leaving the hills and lake shore round Keszthely, the railway curves inland across a small plain to Tapolca, an industrial town and rail junction whose prosperity began with the mining of basalt. The line then swings back to the more pleasant narrow coastal plain.

The line is now approaching the north-eastern end of the lake, which it follows closely before turning sharply inland to the junctions at Casjäg and Szabadbattyán, where the outward route is rejoined.

● **ABOVE LEFT**
A close view at Keszthely of 2-6-2 No. 324-540, of a class dating from 1909, which has just finished a special journey with a train of vintage stock.

● **RIGHT**
The hub of the tram system in Buda is at Moszkva tér, seen here in an "off-peak" period!

FIER TO VLORE, SHKODER TO DURRES

This account of a journey describes a visit made to Albania in the early 1990s during the Communist regime of Enver Hoxha, the fanatical dictator of that small nation. Entry to the country was then exceedingly difficult; the only possible way was to attempt participation in a group tour run by a limited number of, usually, politically minded agencies. Upon arrival, moreover, the riot act was read to all Western visitors; virtually everything worth doing was not only forbidden but "punishable by execution". There was one exception: for travelling the state railway without government permission the penalty was a mere 25 years' hard labour. So one covered the country by rail.

Until the national railway network was inaugurated in 1946, there were only two lines: a 31 km (19 mile) Decauville track taking bitumen from the mine at Selence to Skele, the port 3 km (2 miles) south of Viore; and a much shorter line between

Shkozet and Lakaj, south of Durres. Today passenger-trains run twice daily between Shkoder in the north and Durres, the chief port, via Lezhe and Lac; six times daily between Durres and Eibasan (with one extending to

● **ABOVE**
Vlore Junction. It is from here that asphalt and cement are transported to Durres.

● **BELOW LEFT**
A freight-train waits in the rail yard at Durres.

● **BELOW RIGHT**
A train waits to depart from Tirana station.

INFORMATION BOX

Termini	Fier and Vlore; Shkoder and Durres
Country	Albania
Distance	*c.* 700 km (435 miles)
Date of commencement of construction	1946

● **RIGHT**
The rather elegant, slender structure of the railway bridge near Qukes.

● **BELOW**
The train from Durres arriving at Elbasan. This 30 km (19 miles) of track was opened in 1950.

Pogradec); and twice daily between Durres and Fier; in all some 700 km (435 miles) of track.

A line has long been under construction to link Fier with Vlore, and now, with the help of "volunteer" labour, it is at last complete. However, the much-vaunted connection of the Albanian rail network to the European system south of Titograd in Montenegro has still not materialized. Nor has the link with Bar in Yugoslavia yet been made. Thus the Albanian Railways network remains isolated and detached.

The track is in poor condition, but in 1991 the rolling stock was renewed from Italian sources. Previously most of it originated from Romania, Hungary and the then Czechoslovakia, and the condition was deplorable, with broken seats and overflowing toilets. In fact, even while in operation, the seats and fittings were being used for fuel by chilly passengers and, without the metal replacements, by now there would doubtless have been nothing but the steel bogies left!

Only one class of travel is available, trains are diesel-powered, and because of the mountainous terrain the builders of the line had considerable obstacles to overcome.

The taking of photographs of anything to do with the railway or its routes carried severe penalties, which made the photographs shown on these pages extremely difficult to obtain. As it was, on a second visit, the author was finally arrested for boarding a forbidden train in possession of a camera and was taken before the Ministry of the Interior in Tirana for a severe reprimand and threat of expulsion before being released.

TUNES TO LISBON

The journey commences in Tunes and is a wonderful way to experience the fertile landscape of Portugal. Tunes is a town that has avoided so far the refurbishment or modernization that has afflicted other parts of the network. Much of the investment has come from EU sources, and the accompanying requirements and dictates do not always sit easily with the relaxed local way of life. Welcome track improvements have been made, together with track rationalization and the withdrawal of freight-yards. Expensive and impressive refurbishment of stations has been coupled with de-staffing and the appearance of graffiti and vandalism.

As a junction serving single-track routes to Barreiro, along the Algarve through Faro to the Spanish border and the Algarve branch to Lagos, Tunes sees considerable activity. At times six or more locomotives and four trains may be in the station at once, with complicated shunting of stock between various services. The three-coach train to Lisbon, headed by a French-designed 3,000 hp locomotive, is soon under way, rattling

INFORMATION BOX

Termini	Tunes and Lisbon
Country	Portugal
Distance	259 km (161 miles)
Date of opening	July 1989

● **BELOW**
No. 1933 on train IC582, passing the vineyards in the hills south of Sao Bartolomeu de Messines, having travelled some 11 km (7 miles) from Tunes.

across the turnouts and over the broad level crossing at the Barreiro end of the station. This distinctive crossing, which has a road junction in one arm between the Lagos and main lines, is still operated from a hut by a woman crossing-keeper who shows flags or lights to the train crew as they pass.

The journey provides a great variety of generally sparsely populated landscape ranging from fertile pastures to quite bleak hillsides, that in summer would offer little protection from the sun. Having crossed the flat pastures and small orchards near Tunes, the train soon starts its sinuous course through the first range of hills. Fresh vegetation contrasts with the white walls of isolated farms and the reddish-orange of the soil. In places, grey rock cuttings and cactus bushes add variety.

As the train climbs higher, pockets of mist hang in the hollows, and clear streams and rivers curl around the contours of the hills. Near Sao Marcos da Serra, 27 km (17 miles) from Tunes, the train crosses the Ribeira de Odelouca, from whose banks a deafening chorus of frogs can be heard. Formerly, the hills around here were the harmonious domain of sheep and cork oaks, but increasingly the harsher culture of eucalyptus is becoming dominant. Near

● **OPPOSITE TOP**
The attractive tile-decorated station at
Grandola shows signs of life as the train IC580
rolls in to a stop.

● **RIGHT**
IC583 raises dust from the ballast as it
accelerates through the isolated station of
Santa Clara-Saboia. A line of wagons awaits
the next load of timber in the adjacent siding.

● **RIGHT**
Train IC583, behind
a 1931 Class
locomotive, disturbs
the rural tranquillity
and interrupts the
chorus of frogs,
having crossed the
Ribeira de Odelauca
some 25 km (16
miles) from Tunes.

Pereiras, the train crosses an impressive
stone-arched viaduct, the 123.5 m (405
ft) long Ponte de Mouratos, one of the
tallest structures on the line.

After the train has growled its way
round more curves and through the

station, the landscape, although
undulating, becomes more open. Next
we come to Santa Clara-Saboia, its
attractive station some distance from
either of the communities it purports to
serve, after which the train heads

● **BELOW**
In the tranquil setting of the valley of the
Mouratos, a 1931 Class diesel heads a well-
laden IC582 across the imposing Ponte de
Mouratos viaduct.

● LEFT
The fortified town of
Alcacer do Sol is
seen across the
floodplain of the Rio
Sado as a train
approaches the
274 m (900 ft) long
bridge over the
river. One of the
more distinctive
crops in the area
is rice.

towards the short Tunel da Horta. The
line remains fairly sinuous, providing a
vista of an impressive villa near Torre Va.

More open terrain allows the train to
gather speed. Lighter soils lead to further
variety of vegetation, with pine-woods
and heathland interspersed here and
there. At Alvalade, 111 km (69 miles)
from Tunes, the train encounters orange
orchards and in places lupins abound,
while white egrets, storks and buzzards
can sometimes be seen.

Having left the plain, the train
encounters a lush rolling landscape of
fields and meandering rivers. Broom,
flat-topped pines and firs being tapped
for resin attract the eye before an even
more impressive sight is met. At Alcacer
do Sal, the line takes a broad sweep

● LEFT
Two of the
ubiquitous 1201
Class rest between
duties at the Lisbon
end of Tunes
station.

● BELOW LEFT
SOREFAME-built
No. 1939 thunders
across the points to
the south of Santa
Clara-Saboia, with
IC582 en route to
Barreiro.

around the hilltop town and castle before
crossing the Rio Sado on a girder bridge.
Until a few years ago this view was
absolute perfection, but today it is
marred by a major highway that shares
the locality.

The lazy Rio Sado meanders towards
its estuary, which incorporates one of the
prime wetland nature reserves in the
country. Mudflats, marshland, water
meadows and low wooded hills provide a
rich prospect for both humans and birds.
The line swings away from the water
eventually, and we are back to a sandy
landscape of large fields fringed by cork
oaks and pine.

At Pinheiro, 191 km (119 miles) from
Tunes, the station buildings are well
maintained but somewhat remote from
the tracks – and positively distant from
the community they purport to serve.
Not surprisingly, services are sparse; only
two northbound trains per day are
booked to stop and search for passengers.

From here, the train takes the more
northerly route via Valdera, whereas on
the return journey in the evening it
serves the historic town of Setubal.
Having joined the line serving Vendas

● **RIGHT**
The Fridays-only
Algarve to Porto
sleeping-car express
approaches the
Tunel da Horta,
some 50 km (31
miles) from Tunes,
behind a British-
built 1801 Class.

● **BELOW
RIGHT**
The train IC580
basks in the
morning sun, as it
waits to pass inter-
regional service
IR871 at Grandola.
Not surprisingly
with such a
relatively light load,
the locomotive 1937
has made good time.

displays, not always providing relevant
information, have changed the old
ambience somewhat. There has been talk
of moving the tracks nearer to the new
piers, but not, one hopes, at the expense
of the old station structure.

The ferries provide a frequent and
pleasant voyage across the Tejo (Tagus),
especially if you are able to secure some
of the limited open deck space. The
upper deck was formerly reserved for
first-class passengers, but these days the
accommodation is open to all. Sitting in
the sun at the stern for the half-hour
crossing serves as a welcome appetizer
for lunch. One can watch the activities of
other ferries and catamarans criss-
crossing the harbour and survey the naval
dockyard and commercial yards at
leisure. Dominating all, on a clear day, is
the impressive suspension bridge high
above the waterway.

All too soon the journey is over.
However, just as the Algarve exerts its
annual charms, so too does Lisbon, and
there is no finer way to link the two than
by inter-city express from Tunes and
ferry from Barreiro.

Novas and Casa Branca near Poceirao,
the train races towards the fascinating
junction at Pinhal Novo, which is 233 km
(145 miles) from Tunes. This station still
enjoys an array of semaphore signals and
a commuter service provided, in part, by
elderly ALCO diesels dating from 1948.

On the final stage of the rail journey
to Barreiro, the driver maintains both a
high speed and frequent blasts on the
horn as this area has many official and
unofficial level crossings, as well as
people who use the trackside as an
extended footpath. Barreiro itself boasts
a major locomotive works and extensive
sidings for both locomotives and rolling
stock. The station has an attractive overall
roof and associated metalwork, but
surprisingly few platforms considering
the area it serves.

Until recent years, the ferries to
Lisbon used to depart from jetties

immediately adjacent to the station.
However, as part of a major new
investment, they now leave from opposite
the bus station, a short walk away. New
turnstiles, ticket machines and dot matrix

CALAIS TO MILAN
ACROSS EUROPE BY MEDLOC

Any reference to rail journeys from the Channel coast to Italy conjures up delightful visions of the Orient Express speeding across frontiers while passengers dine on *cordon bleu* meals in Pullman comfort. My own experience, however, as a serviceman in the aftermath of World War II, could hardly have been in greater contrast.

In late March 1946, after a spell of home leave, I reported back to a transit camp outside Southampton, anticipating a return voyage by troopship to Port Said. But the ways of the Military are ever unpredictable, and after whiling away a fortnight, a party of us were bundled aboard a Waterloo-bound train at Southampton Central, hauled by nothing more prestigious than an N Class 2-6-0. On arrival we were promptly transferred to Victoria station, where I had my first glimpse of a West Country Pacific before departing on a semi-fast to Dover Priory. The next day, after a mercifully smooth Channel crossing, we docked at Calais alongside the war-torn remains of the Gare Maritime.

Here I should explain that, to expedite the transit of service personnel between the UK and various Continental destinations, the railway Operating Division of the Royal Engineers had organized the "Medloc" (Mediterranean line of communication) service of troop trains. I was about to experience Route B, which went from Calais to Milan, with feeders onwards to Southern Italy. Route A, meanwhile, linked Dieppe with Toulon, and Route C went from Calais to Villach in Austria. As Route B was discontinued shortly afterwards, I count myself fortunate since, despite the discomforts, it was an unforgettable and unrepeatable journey.

● **RIGHT**
What better locomotive to tackle the gradients between Dijon and Vallorbe than one of the fleet of ex-PLM Mountains? No. 141-F-177 of this large locomotive family is portrayed at Périgueux in 1962.

● **BELOW LEFT**
Haulage of a British troop train was an unusual assignment for a Swiss Federal Railways locomotive, but an Ae4/7, as shown here at Lucerne, was so employed on the Medloc special in April 1946.

● **BELOW RIGHT**
An SNCF Class BB8100 passing through Villeneuve-St-Georges.

The train in which we were to spend the next 37 hours consisted of 11 FS (Italian) corridor coaches – somewhat lacking in such luxuries as upholstery – plus two vans and a silver-painted FS NAAFI car, decorated with army insignia and named Lancastrian for the essential supply of "char and wads" (tea and cake). I was eager for my first sight of a French locomotive, and I was delighted when the former Nord Collin Pacific No. 231-C-43, of a type renowned for pre-war haulage of the Flèche d'Or, backed on to the train. Also in view in the dock area were numerous War Department 2-8-0s awaiting repatriation.

We left Calais around 13.00 and made slow progress, hindered by the vast amount of reconstruction work arising from the ravages of war, along the main line towards Paris. Engines were changed at Amiens. At Boves we had a meal halt, where we were fed and watered beside the line. Another lengthy stop was made at Creil, where a line of 141R Mikado 2-8-2s, newly delivered from America, stood outside the locomotive depot. After the war, a fleet of over 1,300 of

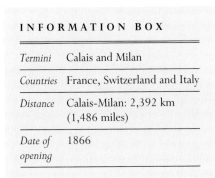

INFORMATION BOX

Termini	Calais and Milan
Countries	France, Switzerland and Italy
Distance	Calais-Milan: 2,392 km (1,486 miles)
Date of opening	1866

SNCF Region 5 (PLM) steam traction. There were Mountains (4-8-2s), including one resplendent in olive green, and a selection of mixed traffic 2-8-2s dating from 1919 onwards, although, curiously, only one example of the fleet of over 300 Pacifics was seen at close quarters. Other attractions included the distinctive French signals, notably "chequerboards" controlled from high cabins designated "Poste 1", "2" etcetera, and goods rolling stock including elderly vans with brakemen's cabins perched high on the ends.

A 2-8-2, No. 141-E-173, took over for the more demanding section to

these rugged machines was to prove of immense help to the SNCF during the years of transition to widespread electrification.

From Creil we diverged from the main line as darkness fell, and my scanty notes tell me that our route thereafter took us through Epluches, Ermont, Eaubonne and round the outskirts of Paris via the North-South Ceinture link line. There were tantalizing glimpses of vast marshalling yards and strange locomotives under the arc lights, including one of the Mallet 031-130TB tanks used for local heavy-freight trains and shunting.

A period of fitful sleep followed – the unyielding seats and persistent draughts were not conducive to slumber, though one enterprising fellow-traveller took to the luggage rack – and daybreak found us making steady progress south-eastwards along the former PLM main line towards Dijon. Superbly engineered, the line closely followed the course of the Yonne and Armençon rivers. This route would in years to come provide a race track for fast expresses such as the Mistral; our speed, however, was restricted to a maximum of around 80 kph (50 mph). Even in a bleary-eyed state, one's interest was soon aroused when passing places such as Laroche-Migennes and Les Laumes-Alésia, both with well-stocked

locomotive depots and busy yards.

During a long halt at Dijon, an important junction where the lines to the Mediterranean and to Switzerland part company, I feasted my eyes on a variety of

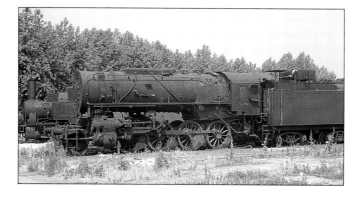

● LEFT
The US Army S160 2-8-0s were invaluable in the haulage of troop trains in Italy during and after the war. This example, as FS No. 736.205, sadly ended its days at Milano Smistamento.

● **RIGHT**
The statue of Victor Emmanuel II in the Piazza
Domo, Milan.

Vallorbe, leaving Dijon at 08.30 and
reaching the Swiss frontier at 15.00.
There was a break in the journey when
we backed up a branch line at Villers-les-
Pots for a meal of stew eaten from our
mess tins at another line-side fast food
outlet. On this section, locomotives
recorded included a 4-8-0 with V-shaped
fronts to the cabs. Most impressive to
British eyes were local passenger 4-8-4
tanks, as big as a pair of LNER N2s
coupled together.

At Vallorbe, a Swiss Federal Railways
Ae4/7 4-8-2 electric locomotive took
over. The next 241 km (150 mile) stretch
was the highlight of the journey. We went
down to Lausanne, then along Lake

Geneva and eastwards through the Rhône
valley to Brigue. The superb scenery
along this section of the route was bathed
in bright sunshine and made a lasting
impression, and a nice touch was that
some of the good citizens of Lausanne

were kind enough to hand us chocolates
while our train waited under the station's
overall glass roof. Even with the addition
of a steam-heating van to an already
heavy train, the 3,120 hp steed gave a
lively performance, non-stop to Brigue,
with the level-crossing bells sounding
merrily as we sped past.

At this time, steam traction had not
been banished from Swiss rails, and a trio
of 4-6-0s and a neat little 2-6-0 had been
observed outside the depot at the end of
Lausanne's platforms. Elsewhere,
however, the scene was all electric with
glimpses of metre-gauge lines at the
stations of Montreux, Aigle and
St-Maurice. As twilight fell we threaded
the Simplon tunnel, emerging at the
other end into Italy.

During a prolonged stop, another
meal was consumed at Domodossola
before departure for Milan at 21.00
behind FS Pacific No. 601.010. This
locomotive, rather more impressive in
looks than in performance, was one of
only 33 built just prior to World War I.
With modifications in the 1930s, most
FS main-line passenger work was
entrusted to the more numerous and
dependable Compound 2-6-2s.

Little was seen during the run to
Milan, where we arrived in darkness at
the great 22-platform terminus at the
unsociable hour of 02.00.

● **RIGHT**
The Gallerie
Emanuelle in Milan.

● **OPPOSITE
BOTTOM**
The FS Italia electric
locomotive, which
took over at
Domodossola, was a
1-Do-1, identical
with No. E428-028,
recorded at the
same station 15
years later.

MYRDAL TO FLÅM
THE FLÅM RAILWAY

The Flåm Railway, part of the Norwegian State Railway system, or Norges Statsbaner (NSB), runs between the towns of Myrdal and Flåm, a distance of 20 km (12 miles). The railway's claim to fame lies in the fact that Myrdal is 865 m (2,838 ft) higher than Flåm, making this line one of the world's steepest non-rack-operated railways. Since the late 1950s, NSB has been selling an excursion ticket called "Norway in a Nutshell" for a round trip from Bergen by train, boat and bus via the Flåm railway. This is the journey described.

However, before boarding a train, a little history of the Flåm railway. Flåmdalen – the Flåm valley – starts from Myrdal with a 350 m (1,148 ft) drop, and it is this that causes the major engineering work as the railway must negotiate it by tunnels, ledges and hairpin curves. The first survey for the line was in 1893, which produced a proposal for an 18 km (11 mile), 3 ft 6 in gauge rack railway with gradients of 10 per cent on the rack section. However, after

● **BELOW**
Preserved electric locomotive No. 9.2063 of 1944, on display at Flåm. Adjacent is the old station building, which houses a small museum about the Flåm railway.

● **BELOW**
NSB electric locomotive No. 11.2110 at Flåm on the stock of the overnight sleeper service to Oslo. This is the Flåm branch's only through train to the rest of the network, the coaches being attached to the overnight Bergen to Oslo train. The Flåm branch is one of the last outposts of the Class 11 locomotives.

government approval, the plan was modified to the current, standard-gauge, electrified adhesion route in 1923. The purpose of the line was to link the Bergen to Oslo line, itself completed in 1909, with the Sognefjord. This route was already popular with tourists, although the limit was one person per chaise on the uphill journey, limiting the number of people that could be handled.

The Flåm railway has a ruling gradient of 5.5 per cent for 80 per cent of the line's length. There are 20 tunnels totalling 5,692 m (over 3½ miles), which is over a quarter of the line. The minimum curve radius is 130 m (427 ft). All trains operating over this line are fitted with five different braking systems, each of which alone can stop the train. Unsurprisingly, maximum speed is limited, to 40 kph (25 mph), giving a journey time of 53 minutes. However, the scenery is so spectacular, that this seems too short a time, not too long!

It had been intended to open the railway in 1942, but wartime measures meant it was opened in August 1940,

● **RIGHT**
A view from Stalheim Hotel, towards
Gudvangen and the Nærøyfjord. The pass road
leaves the new road where it crosses the
stream in the middle of the photograph, and
then crosses the stream a little to the right.

although steam-operated. The electric
locomotives ordered, on the other hand,
were delayed by the war, not arriving
until 1947. These locomotives,
designated Class E19, survived until
1984. One has been put on display at
Flåm station.

Despite threats of closure in the
1960s, traffic on the line has grown,
reaching 315,000 in 1992. The passenger
service is seasonal, with only four trains
operating each way in winter, but 12
services each way in summer.

The day's journey starts from the
terminus station in Bergen, Norway's
second city. This is an imposing stone-
fronted and very solid-looking building
with a curved roof over the four main
tracks. The journey to Myrdal is by

INFORMATION BOX

THE FLÅM RAILWAY

Termini	Myrdal and Flåm
Country	Norway
Distance	20 km (12 miles)
Date of opening	1940

● **RIGHT**
Fylkesbaatane's boat
Skagastol arriving at
Flåm. Its previous
use as a car ferry
can be discerned,
the raisable bow
continuing to be
used for embarking.

stopping train, which is formed of a
suburban electric multiple unit (EMU).
These are not as comfortable as the long-
distance trains, but the low seat-backs
and large windows allow good views of
the passing scenery.

While the journey to Myrdal is not as
spectacular as the Flåm railway, nor the
countryside as barren as that on the
central part of the Oslo to Bergen railway,
there are some very attractive views on
the first 86 km (53 miles) to Voss. Best
of all is the stretch between Takvam and

NSB three-car EMU No. 69625 at Myrdal, having worked from Bergen.

Stanghelle, where the railway follows one of the minor fjords.

From Voss, the railway starts to climb. The line to Oslo will reach 1,300 m (4,265 ft) above sea level at its highest point, but this journey only goes as far as Myrdal, 867 m (2,845 ft), two hours and 135 km (84 miles) from Bergen.

Myrdal is situated between two tunnels and seems to exist purely for the purposes of a railway junction. The only visible habitations are a few houses, quite probably built by the railway. The steepness of the Flåm railway is obvious from the start, when one sees the way the railway track disappears downhill from the end of the platform. During the journey, anyone walking up and down the carriage – literally – will realize just how steep the track is, one end of the 24 m (79 ft) coach being 1.4 m (4½ ft) below the other.

The first view comes after one kilometre (⅔ mile) at Vatnahalsen, where the Kjosfossen power-station lake and waterfall can be seen below. Three kilometres (2 miles) later, the train stops at Kjosfossen to allow passengers to leave the train and photograph the waterfall, now pouring down from several hundred feet above.

A couple of kilometres (1.24 miles) later, the highest settlement in the Flåmdalen comes into view. At several points, between tunnels and snow shelters, spectacular views are available, both down and upwards, where you can see parts of the route taken by the railway. In particular, the "window" out from one of the tunnels inside the rock face can be seen above the snow shelter on the lower level of the line. At Berekvam, slightly under half-way, there is a passing loop, the only place on the line where trains can pass each other. Below Dalsbotn, Flåm church can be seen along with some farms in the flatter valley floor. Soon after Hareina, the gradient slackens as the valley floor is reached, and the last couple of kilometres are relatively flat, passing through farmlands, but still overhung by the towering sides of the fjord. The "port" of Flåm is finally reached after negotiating a narrowing and curving of the valley, such that the fjord cannot be seen from the train on the journey down from Myrdal.

The area around Flåm station is clearly aimed at tourists, with a number of gift shops and restaurants. However, a short walk brought relief from the throng! The two-hour connection is more than adequate to see the area around the railway station and, with a little effort, there may be enough time to walk some way up the valley towards the Flåm church. Some of this time should be spent on a visit to the interesting Flåm railway museum, situated in the old station building, which explains the history of this extraordinary railway.

A view of Flåmdalen from below Dalsbotn, seen from a train on the Flåm railway. Flåm church is in the small settlement in the middle of the view. The Aurlandfjord is off to the right after the valley narrows.

● **LEFT**
A view of a small
hamlet on the shores
of the Nærøyfjord.

● **BELOW LEFT**
A view of the sheer
rock face that the
Flåm railway must
negotiate, seen from
the train below
Kjosfossen. Both
visible galleries are
on the Flåm railway.
The first stretch
from Myrdal to
Vatnahalsen is out of
sight, higher up.

● **BELOW
RIGHT**
NSB battery electric
shunter No. 207.3
outside Flåm depot.

Preserved electric locomotive No.
9.2063, of the type built for the Flåm
line, is displayed on the station platform.
The adjacent small railway depot is home
to an unusual battery shunting
locomotive.

Gudvangen is on the Nærøyfjord, a
branch off the Aurlandfjord. The village
appears to be little more than a couple of
farms, a jetty for the ferries and a tourist
shop and restaurant, albeit in an
attractive setting.

From here our trip continues by coach
to Voss. The coach trip is dramatic in

itself. The first section is along the valley
at the end of the fjord, but the coach
turns off the main road to take the pass
road up to Stalheim. This road is very
narrow and steep and has frequent
hairpin bends. These are a struggle for
the coach, even without the distraction of
downhill traffic. This is fortunately light,
as a new road tunnel has been
constructed to avoid this section. The
views from the coach are spectacular, but
are as nothing compared to those from
Stalheim. This is a hotel perched on a
saddle between two valleys. On one side

is the steep drop down to Gudvangen; on
the other, the much shallower drop
towards Vinje.

The run on to Voss is much less
dramatic. The scenery is no less
attractive, although the height of the land
allows only a minimal amount of
vegetation to grow, which shows one a
different side to the country. Voss is a
lakeside town and skiing centre, with an
imposing church. It used to be the
junction for a branch line to the
Hardangerfjorden, since closed. Finally, a
train is joined for the return to Bergen.

● **ABOVE**
**The Glacier Express, on one of the world's
most spectacular scenic railway journeys,
Gornergrat to St Moritz, Switzerland.**